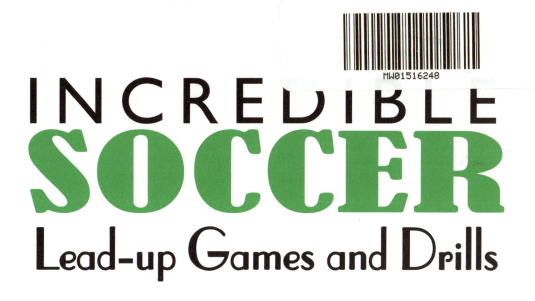

INCREDIBLE
SOCCER
Lead-up Games and Drills

John Vidovich Jim Lefkos

**Faculty of Physical Education and Health
University of Toronto**

Sport Books Publisher

Graphics and design by Takao Tsuruoka and My1 Designs

National Library of Canada Cataloguing in Publication Data

Vidovich, John
   Incredible soccer lead-up games and drills

ISBN 0-920905-73-0

1. Soccer – Training. I. Lefkos, Jim II. Title.

GV943.9.T7V58 2002   796.334   C2002-900846-8

Pictures reproduced with permission from the Faculty of
Physical Education and Health, University of Toronto.
Photo credits: Mark Brownson, Lewko Hryhorijiw, Bridget Bates

Distribution world-wide by
Sport Books Publisher
278 Robert Street
Toronto, ON M5S 2K8
Canada

http://www.sportbookspub.com
E-mail: sbp@sportbookspub.com
Fax: 416-966-9022

Printed in the United States

CONTENTS

PART I

EFFECTIVE COACHING METHODS

Peter Klavora, University of Toronto

The basic idea of coaching soccer is the development of players' technical and tactical skills as well as his or her physical and psychological abilities. As a result, each of these components should be carefully developed during practice. These abilities and skills are initially tested in practice and training games, where conditions can be controlled and monitored, before moving on to more important competitive situations that serve as tests for future performance potential. The goal of practice should be to develop consistent performance during competition, which is vital for success.

There is a growing body of research on a wide range of learning and coaching principles that make coaching soccer effective. Eight of these concepts, designed to enhance the methodology of coaching soccer are presented in this section. They deal with (1) the systematic analysis of the soccer task; (2) skill presentation techniques; (3) the understanding of the athlete's limitations in processing information; (4) the importance of feedback in effective coaching; (5) the appreciation of the learning stages; (6) coaching tactics; (7) developing competition smartness; and (8) the need to plan an all-year training program.

Task analysis

Any soccer skill can be broken down into a set of component movements which are quite distinct from each other in terms of the operations needed to produce an effective performance. The component movements of the task are envisaged as the *subroutines* involved in the total performance. Together, the subroutines form the overall task which is conceived as an *executive plan*. This executive plan then is the overall goal, aim, or, objective the player is trying to master; at the same time it serves as an organizational process that controls the order in which a sequence of simpler tasks or movements is carried out.

Each subroutine can be further broken down into simpler movements, the *sub-subroutines*. The process of division depends upon the complexity of the task at hand. It stops when all basic movements that comprise the task are identified.

It is advantageous, therefore, for the coach to break down each of the soccer tasks into basic movements, ordered from the simplest to the most complex in a hierarchical fashion. Once these hierarchies are formed, the player can easily be introduced to new material at the level most appropriate given his or her past experience. The drill section of the book displays nine charts that present skill hierarchies for all soccer tasks. Obviously, the less experienced a player, the lower in the hierarchy he or she should begin. Once the basic movements are mastered, the player can attempt movements at the next level in the task hierarchy structure. This process is continued until the most complex movements of the soccer task are learned.

When learned, the skills at the bottom of each task hierarchy become mainly automatic and "run off" without much attention by the player. Once they are mastered, these movements are relegated to the lower centres of the brain and do not overload the player's nervous system. Through practices using numerous lead-up games and drills, the execution of well-learned skills becomes automatic.

Skill presentation techniques

The best way to introduce a new skill is demonstration coupled with an explanation of the skill. If the coach does not possess the skill, it can be demonstrated by an athlete or an assistant coach. Other visual forms of visual information can be used, such as still pictures of proper actions, film clips or videos of successful performances, etc. The instruction should be kept brief and to the point, emphasizing only one or two key points at a time. Furthermore, the teaching formation must be such that all athletes are in front of the demonstrator and have a good view from the right angle. Several lead-up games and drills designed to develop the same skill must be selected very carefully as to assure the right progression in skill development and to prevent boredom. Furthermore, the selected drills should challenge the skill level of the athletes. If drills are too easy, the players may become bored quickly. Conversely, if the drills are too difficult, the athletes may become frustrated with lack of progress in skill development.

Understanding the player as an information processor

Coaches seldom realize that most coaching principles are based on knowledge of athletes' limitations and capacities in receiving and processing information. After a poor performance it many coaches begin a long lecture about which bone does what and what muscles to use and at what particular time in the movement this or that muscle is to be activated. In essence, such coaches are observing and commenting only on the end result – the response of a whole series of interior processes that go on while the player is trying to execute the new skill at his or her very best. What are these processes?

Psychomotor processes (**Figure 1**) are part of the player's nervous system and are, in most cases, taken for granted. These mechanisms help the learner to sense, perceive,

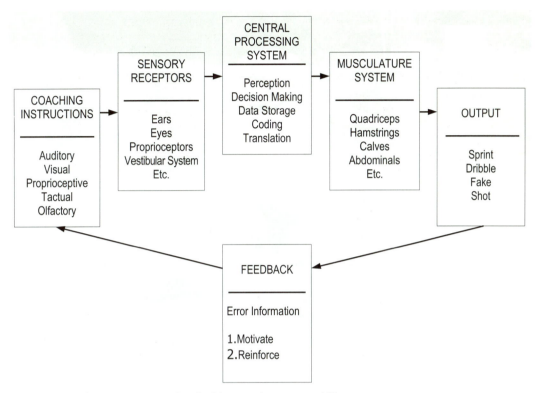

Figure 1 Psychomotor processes involved in executing a soccer skill.

attend to, store or memorize, decide, and organize an action in relationship to the demands placed on him by the coach and the environment. These mechanisms transmit information that is flowing between the athlete and the coach. However, these mechanisms are full of limitations that dictate our coaching approaches and teaching strategies. By keeping these limitations in mind, the coach becomes more effective which in turn helps players to progress faster. **Table 1** (see page 10) outlines some of the major limitations of an athlete's psychomotor system and main coaching strategies to overcome these limitations.

It is difficult to separate the player's sensory capacities from his perceptual processes. What input the athlete actually processes is highly dependent upon the quality of her sensory and perceptual mechanisms. In practice the athlete is constantly bombarded with stimuli coming in through various senses. These stimuli are provided externally by the coach and internally by proprioceptors (receptors in the muscles, tendons, ligaments, and vestibule sense). However, the player's single-channel system or selective attention that serves as a funnel gates out most of the available information presented to him. If the coach wants the player to perceive, i.e., hear or see, the right things, he would

Table 1 Characteristics of an athlete's psychomotor processes and coaching strategies.

MECHANISM	LIMITATION	COACHING STRATEGY
Sensory Mechanisms	• Poor visual skills, such as dynamic visual acuity • Athlete does not hear instructions	• Detect vision problems early • Limit noise in the gym; speak clearly and loudly
Perceptual Mechanisms	• One-track mind; selective attention; can attend to only one major point	• Provide only one critical component of a skill at a time
Short-term Memory	• Limited capacity • Significant rate of loss • Can be easily interfered with	• Provide only a limited amount of information; do not overload athlete • Minimize time between demonstration and rehearsal of skill • Avoid unrelated activities in gym, such as workers in the background, spectators yelling or commenting, other teams practicing, etc.
Long-term or Permanent Memory	• Must rehearse to encode and retain information	• Provide continuing rehearsal of skill until it is learned properly
Player's Psychological State	• Anxiety • Attention and fatigue • Boredom	• Provide non-threatening learning environment • Avoid practicing new skills when fatigued • Introduce new drills to coach same skill

have to select and present instructions carefully so that they have a chance to get through for interpretation and recognition. The single-channel system, selective attention, and short term memory are limitations of the player's perceptual mechanism that every coach must consider for optimal learning results in practice.

Importance of feedback in effective coaching

The coach's instructions, corrections, explanations, interpretations, comments, or notes, directed to the player during practice, evaluate her current performance. This evaluation is the feedback that systematically shapes the player's movements into the desired act, according to the coach's plan. According to motor-learning texts, "Practice alone does not make perfect, practice with appropriate feedback makes perfect... Feedback is probably the single most important factor during practice sessions." This and similar quotations indicate the significance of the presence of meaningful feedback in learning and performance.

The coach's feedback can be either *descriptive* or *prescriptive* in nature. A descriptive feedback statement indicates something about what the player did ("not so good on the follow through," "try better at next attempt," etc.); it presumes that the player knows what to do on the next attempt. Prescriptive feedback, on the other hand, provides the athlete with information he or she can use to make more effective corrections in their subsequent attempt ('focus on the wrist at the point of release') at the task. In general, prescriptive feedback is considered more effective than descriptive feedback.

There are four fundamental questions concerning the efficacy of coach's provision of feedback: (1) when is feedback most beneficial; (2) how much feedback is necessary; (3) how precise should feedback be; (4) what should the timing of feedback be; and (5) motivation properties of feedback.

Stages of learning and feedback The coach's feedback is especially vital early in the learning process. Later in his or her training, however, after he or she has gained experience and developed an internalized model of the correct soccer skill or task which he or she uses as a reference pattern, the coach's attention can be reduced and eventually completely withdrawn.

How much feedback is necessary The earlier discussion about the athlete as an information processor should answer the question of how much feedback is necessary for an effective instruction process. Particularly during coaching of novel skills or plays, an athlete's 'one-track mind' can process and attend to only a limited amount of information. The athlete can effectively concentrate on only one novel movement. Only later, when he or she becomes familiar with the novel task, can he or she shift her attention to other novel tasks and/or share the attention with other requirements of the movement or play. Although the athlete is limited in his capacities to process the coach's information, intense but selective coaching is nevertheless required in the early stages of the player's development if he or she is to progress at an optimal rate. In other words, no more and no less information about a performance should be provided than the athlete is capable of handling. The instruction must be adjusted to the amount of information the player can use.

How precise should feedback be Motor learning research has suggested that precise coaching generates far better results than any other type. The coach must formulate a precise standard of each task or play he wants to coach. Then, he or she must develop a trained eye in order to be able to provide precise information to the athlete abut his errors and how to correct them.

To decrease the dependency of athletes on coach's feedback as they become more skilled the coach may consider using *bandwidth* feedback. With this method, the coach only gives feedback when an athlete's movements fall outside some acceptable level of correctness, or bandwidth. This type of feedback has many advantages. The coach gives feedback less frequently and athletes' intrinsic feedback gains in importance which allows them to strengthen their permanent memory of the skill or play.

Timing of feedback To consider the timing of the coach's feedback to the athlete is to apply his short-term memory limitations to the coaching situation. Short-term memory bank is very susceptible to loss, and generally the greater the delay before giving the athlete information about her performance, the less effect the given information has. Thus, an intense, continuous instruction is more beneficial to the development of skills than the provision of coaching at the end of practice when the team is ready to leave the field.

Motivation properties of feedback The coach's encouraging words 'good,' 'excellent,' 'that's it,' etc., not only provide the athlete with information about her performance, but also act as a reinforcement. When the player is given precise information about his technique, this feedback strengthens the correct response. In this regard the coach's instruction increases motivation, and, in general, information about one's performance affects the incentive to do well. It is encouraging for the player to hear that he or she is improving. The improvements make the athlete happy and motivate him to maintain her interest and his desire to keep practicing. Thus, the coach's feedback fulfills a valuable motivational role. (see **Figure 1,** page 9)

Learning stages

Technical and tactical training play a central role in developing a complete player. Technical elements of the game are normally developed in three stages of learning: acquisition, stability, and application.

Acquisition stage The goal of this learning stage is to introduce new technical elements to players and have them perform the skills in simplified conditions, initially while standing, and later with movement. When introducing a skill for the first time, it is important that the coach introduces it in a simplified setting. Initially, rough forms of the skill are developed in relatively simple conditions. The player's performance is highly variable and he or she is generally not aware of exactly what should be done differently the next time to improve. As a result, he or she needs specific information that will assist him or her in correcting what he or she has done wrong. With some practice, the player moves on to the second (stabilization) learning stage.

Stabilization stage The main objective of the stabilization stage is to refine their skills. The errors are fewer and less significant. The players are developing an ability to detect some of their own errors in performing the various tasks and various game elements. This provides the athletes with some specific guidelines about how to continue practice. Variability of performance from one attempt to another also begins to decrease.

Gradually, the coach introduces variations according to game demands. Variations can be with regards to movement speed (ball or player), distance, movement direction, etc. Scoring should be attempted during high speed, from different distances, from different angles, and, if necessary, from both, left and right, directions. An important step is to practice game-specific combinations where several game elements are combined into a more demanding practice. Initially, one should choose combination elements that occur immediately before or after the skill just learned. Then, the easiest form should be chosen (depending on the game) and should be practiced in more demanding complex game forms. When practicing dribbling, e.g., receiving the ball while standing or running can be added, and after dribbling, playing the ball to another player can be added.

In order to further strengthen technical abilities, one has to include opponents, whose impact is guided by the coach. Initially the skill should be practiced with inanimate opponents (objects) and then with passive opponents (players). The player has to learn to take an opponent into account. The passive opponent eventually turns into a semi-active opponent that agitates the player but still lets him finish the exercise. The player now has to broaden his technical abilities in order to be successful.

The demands get even higher, when the opponent becomes an active opponent that not only tries to disturb the flow of movement but also tries to hinder it. At this point tactical training becomes important and must be introduced into practice gradually.

Application stage After much practice and experience with various skills, the athlete moves into the application stage of learning. Here, skills have become almost automatic or habitual. The player does not have to attend to the entire production of the skill but has learned to perform most of the skill without thinking about it at all.

The application stage is the result of a tremendous amount of practice; it allows players to produce soccer skills and movements without concentrating on the entire movement. Therefore, they are able to attend to other aspects of the game, such as tactics. The goal of practice becomes learning how to apply the learned technical elements and the game's complex combinations in a game situation within a determined tactical framework. Thus, learning of tactical skills becomes a very important aspect of practice in the application learning stage.

Coaching tactics

The development of tactical abilities is a complicated process because it consists of a multi-layered system of sub-processes that normally develop in three steps:

Step 1 This step is mainly concerned with strengthening of individual and collective tactical methods and variations to solve a specific tactical problem. This includes training of individual movement forms and team combinations with the goal to use them at the right time at the right place, either alone or with other players.

An example of an individual attack tactic is to "get past a player with a ball." To solve this problem there are several basic forms with variations that can be practiced; initially without an opponent, then with a passive opponent and a half-active opponent. Basic forms include: (1) to get past a player while moving with change of pace; (2) to get past a player from a standing position using an attack fake; (3) to get past a player from a standing position using a passing fake; and (4) to get past a player from a standing position with body fakes.

These basic play forms and their variations should be introduced one after the other and practiced diligently with the main goal to strengthen their correct execution.

Step 2 The second step involves perceptual and cognitive tasks where the players are learning to correctly assess a game situation and then correctly respond to the specific demand of the game. This requires learning to make quick and good judgments with a semi-active or active opponent.

The player has to learn to recognize a specific game situation or even create it, in order to use certain tactical elements. For this type of training, lead-up games that closely simulate competition situations can be effectively employed. Various forms of lead-up games are still easier to play compared to scrimmage practice, or competition games (fewer players, fewer opponents, smaller field area, etc.).

Step 3 The goal of this step is the correct application of the acquired basic forms and variations in a game. The tasks of this step are to develop the abilities to use tactics in the right situations, and also to develop the ability to create situations where a certain tactic can be used. The latter should be practiced under simpler conditions and in scrimmage practice, so that they can be applied appropriately in actual games. In some cases, the practice conditions should be harder than in actual competition.

Developing competition smartness

Training of competition smartness should occupy an important part of teams practice. It is mainly developed by playing competitive games under four progressively more demanding conditions: (1) simplified conditions; (2) scrimmage practice; (3) very demanding conditions; and (4) competition.

Practice games played under simplified conditions This introductory level of competition is characterized by playing simplified preparatory games using half field, smaller goals, reduced number of players or uneven number of players, simplified rules, etc. This results in lower technical requirements. Initially, only simple technical skills are required. With regard to tactics, individual and simple group tactical actions are predominant (**Table 2**).

Table 2 Practice games played under simplified conditions.

RULES	TECHNIQUE	TACTICS
• Fewer main rules • Shorter play time • Altered number of players: ⟹ Fewer players ⟹ One-sided player advantage • Scaled-down equipment: ⟹ Smaller goals ⟹ Half field	• Simple technical skills and abilities required	• Easy tactical applications in attack and defense: ⟹ Mainly individual tactical acts ⟹ Simple group tactical acts

Scrimmage practice Scrimmage practice involves practice games within the own team, with full number of players and regular game rules. From scrimmage to scrimmage, the coach progressively increases the demands by introducing more rules, increasing playing time, and demanding higher intensity of play. Each player should be provided with plenty of opportunities to apply the acquired skills in scrimmage practice. Furthermore, it is important to work on the gradual elimination of technical mistakes.

Another purpose of scrimmage games is to practice the individual and group tactical elements that were practiced in training. In scrimmage practice, the coach has the possibility to interrupt the game and point out mistakes and explain or demonstrate certain aspects or situations. Each player is assigned very specific goals which they are encouraged to apply during practice games.

The constant development and refinement of individual and group tactical elements, as well as the conscious application of these elements during scrimmage practice, lead to a constantly higher quality of play. The coach must insure that all players have an equal opportunity to play during this stage of development.

Practice games played under more demanding conditions In order to prepare players really well, we recommend practicing games under more demanding conditions. These games provide greater challenge than the standard of competition games. This can be done with regard to physical, tactical, technical, or psychological aspects, but often, the increase of one aspect makes the other aspects harder, too. Table 3 (see page 16) shows a few possibilities. When planning games under more demanding conditions, the coach must take into account several factors, such as skill and fitness level of the athletes, the team's tactical abilities, etc. It is important that the players are able to effectively meet more demanding conditions.

Table 3 Practice games played under more demanding conditions.

PHYSICAL ASPECT	TECHNICAL ASPECT	TACTICAL ASPECT	PSYCHOLOGICAL ASPECT
• Longer play time	• Decreasing goal size	• One-sided team superiority	• Providing high noise background
• Fewer no. of players	• Altering no. of players	• Playing against much stronger opponent	• Playing game after physical exhaustion
• Strenuous tactical demands	• Playing with weaker foot only	• Playing game with four goals	• Giving one-sided instructions
• Carrying weighted vests, weighted wrist bands, etc. during play		• Making higher tactical demands, etc.	• Demanding additional training

Competition games played under normal conditions Successful competition is the goal of all coaching efforts. The players have to demonstrate how successfully they can apply their acquired technical and tactical skills and whether their technical, tactical, physical and psychological preparation was thorough enough. It is important to find the right tactical concept with its specific variations and to apply it, based on the performance ability of one's own team and of the opponents, as well as their strategy. Competition games should be evaluated thoroughly and conclusions should be drawn for future training.

Planning an all-year training program

Overall planning of training aims at producing the highest possible individual performance. Since this can be achieved only after many years of preparation, intermediate goals must be set, guaranteeing a systematic build-up of performance. Planning thus comprises: Long-term development plans and multi-year plans for individual development stages, annual plans, and plans for specific periods and stages within an annual plan, such as preparation for a tournament, tapering for playoffs, etc.

The master plan To achieve optimal performance in players and the team, an all-year training program must be adopted. Only a carefully planned annual plan over an entire year will assure an optimal development of the athletes' physical and psychological capabilities and skills. No matter what level it is for, an annual plan should contain the following: goals and tasks for each player; performance goals for the team; dates for testing of skills, fitness medical examination, and competitions; specific plans for skill, tactics and fitness training; and a clear division of the year into sub-phases.

Table 4 An example of a master plan for a North American professional outdoor season.

DATES	DEC-JAN	FEB	MAR	APR	MAY-SEP	OCT	NOV
PERIOD-IZATION	Transition	Preparation		Competition			
	Transition	General Preparation	Specific Preparation	Pre-Competition	Competi-tion	Taper	Playoff

(NOTE: For more detailed information on periodization, refer to the book, *Periodization Theory and Methodology of Training*, by Tudor Bompa. Human Kinetics, 1999)

The master plan must assure a systematic development of training throughout the year until the peak of the competitive season, the playoffs. Detailed division of the plan into shorter periods, also known as *periodization of training*, helps the coach maintain tight control over the continuous improvement of the athletes' performance. The various phases in the annual plan, the preparation, competitive and transitory phase, are determined on the basis of the most important competitions in the season. For most teams, these competitions include respective playoffs (**Table 4**).

The preparation period The main objectives during the preparation period is to create fitness, technical, and tactical prerequisites for further increase in team's performance during the subsequent competitive period. The preparation period includes a general physical preparation period and a soccer-specific period. Each period lasts approximately six to eight weeks.

The competitive period The competitive period is divided into pre-competition, main competition, tapering, and playoffs competition periods. The principal task of pre-competition period is to convert all basic capacities of the preparation period into competitive performance. The pre-competition period may include the training camp, and exhibition schedules. The main competition period includes the regularly scheduled league games. A short tapering period may be scheduled just before the playoff competition period, the concluding part of the season, begins.

The transition period The transition period commences immediately after the conclusion of the competitive period and may last up to a month. During this period, the players are taking a break from soccer-related training but should regularly cross train to maintain a good general fitness level.

PART II

MOTIVATION & INSPIRATION

Peter Klavora, University of Toronto

Motivation in athletes is the key to their effective learning of skills and persistent training at high levels of intensity. It is considered to be the intangible that makes the difference between successful and unsuccessful participation in competition.

One of the most important roles played by the coach is that of motivator. The coach's personality, attitudes and convictions, his goals and motivational strategies are of primary importance to the development of interest, motivation, and attitudes of his players toward training and competition. All of these, in turn, affect the degree of success the athlete will achieve. Therefore, the coach must make an effort to understand the motivational forces that stimulate an individual's athletic participation. The coach must realize that there are different sources of motivation that direct a youngster into the game of soccer and that later incite him to work long and hard toward achieving success in competition. The coach must accept the fact that his athletes' reasons for participation differ greatly. Therefore, the coach must (1) make an effort to know and understand each player's specific needs, interests, and motives related to participation in soccer; (2) know the various assessment techniques which will help him identify his athletes' motives; and (3) learn and study the various motivational techniques and strategies designed to motivate players.

The coach as a motivator

The coach's ability to motivate his athletes is essential because, when all factors are fairly equal, teams who succeed are those who are *the most highly motivated during practices* and those who are also mentally well prepared for competition. When the coach is able to instill a burning desire to succeed in a team, that team will be the hardest-working unit. In other words, if properly motivated, the team will always train hard as long as necessary; this in turn leads to competitive success.

The affection and respect the coach succeeds in generating within the team have always been among the greatest motivators in keeping an athlete working hard in practice. This affection and respect of his athletes must be earned by demonstrating not only a solid technical knowledge, but also a number of personal qualities that make the coach effective in handling and working with the team. A well-liked coach (1) sets the right mood for practice—this mood is confident and relaxed; (2) is interested in his athletes' overall development and not merely in their athletic achievement; (3) is not an authoritarian nor is he excessively permissive. He sets reasonable rules for practice and is consistent in enforcing them; (4) is a hard worker, well organized, and tries very hard to make the training environment a pleasant place where athletes usually stay for several hours a day; (5) tries to be supportive and understanding because athletes often arrive at practice tired and weary after a long day of studying and/or work. The coach's smile and concern help the athlete to forget his problems more quickly and to settle into an effective practice.

There is no one way for the coach to earn the aforementioned affections since the personalities of coaches vary. Every effective coach provides leadership that is unique and suited to his personality. However, effective leadership also results from several standardized motivational techniques that can be learned.

Motivation for practice

Every player on the team must develop training discipline and an ability to push oneself to the maximum at every practice. These psychological qualities can be acquired only if the player becomes involved in soccer through a highly motivated program. Such a program makes each athlete approach practice with zest and eagerness and makes each athlete look forward to practice with anticipation. The daily practice becomes an entertaining and satisfying experience which challenges the team intellectually as well as physically. This positive attitude does not happen accidentally; it is the result of a carefully planned motivational program designed by the coach. The program must include several specific, carefully selected procedures that are highly motivational and that incite the team to ever greater training demands. Such a program develops pride in athletes about their acquired skills and physical fitness.

Useful motivational strategies

There are many motivational strategies that have been used effectively in many successful programs. It is not expected that a coach will be able to introduce into his program all of the techniques suggested here, but by incorporating a few into the ones he already practices the coach can expect a positive reaction and a heightened   enthusiasm from his players.

Educating the athlete The contemporary practice on any level of participation taxes the athlete physically and mentally. The athlete who understands the purpose of each phase of his training will give the coach more cooperation and will be more motivated during each practice session than the one who is completely uninformed. Therefore, the coach is wise to take time to explain to the team such concepts as (1) skill biomechanics; (2) the principles of various training methods and the effect on the athlete's physiological adaptation; (3) peaking phenomena; (4) the overload principles of training, etc.

The education of players can be done at regular team meetings. These meetings should be very carefully planned. Such matters as the progress of the team, training plans for the next phase, and the review of the videotapes should also be discussed. Athletes' concerns could also be aired at such meetings in order that the athletes be involved in the program intellectually as well as physically.

The education of athletes should be an ongoing process, before, during, and after practices, when the coach reviews the purpose of these practices and justifies his daily coaching methods. A brief comment or statement, hardly longer than a sentence, often does the job.

Variety in training Contemporary training is a demanding activity, requiring many hours of work from the athlete. The volume and intensity of training are continuously increasing, and the players repeat drills and technical elements numerous times. This, unfortunately, may lead to monotony and boredom, which negatively effects team's motivation. Therefore, the coach needs to be creative, with knowledge of a large resource of drills that allow developing skills and movements of similar technical pattern. The coach's capacity to create, to be inventive, and to work with imagination is an important advantage for successful variety in training. Only the coach's imagination limits the variety of activity, which can be introduced into daily training. However, it is important that the designed training program follows some general principles that guarantee the necessary short- and long-range goals.

Self-planned workouts One aspect of successful coaching is to develop self-reliance in athletes. To develop this quality and to further motivate practice sessions the coach may, on a given day every week, let a team member plan the entire or part of the workout for the team within certain guidelines. The 'self-planned workouts' procedure adds to the variety in training and reinforces the education of athletes. This certainly increases motivation for practice because athletes perceive that they are responsible for their own actions as they become more involved.

Rewards as motivators The coach can set up a reward system that provides symbols of recognition for a practice well done. The system can provide great incentive in practice for most players, since athletes generally demonstrate a considerable need for recognition. The rewards for special achievements can be simple. The coach may award special hats or shirts to the most improved player of the week; or, each week the coach may let the athlete who worked the hardest wear a specially colored shirt; or the player who scores the winning goal in a scrimmage receives a pound of jelly beans. Again, the only limitation in setting a successful reward system is a coach's imagination.

It is amazing how much motivation within the team this kind of costless reward system generates. It adds a great deal to the quality of practice as most players try very hard to earn at least one such award here and there. It is important, however, that the reward system be set up in such a way that even the less gifted players can experience some measure of success. It boosts their spirit enormously and lets them know that they too are important and necessary members of the team.

Performance evaluation   Regular performance evaluation throughout the year keeps most athletes enthusiastic and motivated for daily practice at the desired intensity levels. The performance evaluation provides the athlete with the necessary feedback about his own progress from test to test and from year to year. Continuous progress is one of the strongest motivators to an athlete. Achieving short- and long-term goals gives him a tremendous sense of accomplishments which drives him even harder in practice.

Performance evaluation provides the coach with the necessary feedback about the effectiveness of his program as well. Continuous progress of most team members from test to test is an indication of well-designed program and a highly motivated team. Additionally, the test scores provide a useful ranking of the athletes and can be used for selection of the team or starting players.

Setting team and individual goals   The establishment of goals and consequent training programs to achieve them is another strong form of motivation that leads to greater zest for training. There exist two types of goals: *team goals* and *individual goals*. Both are equally important. Initially, individual goals are more important since each individual really wants to see an improvement. He or she must see regular progress in order to want to continue; these goals, if well set, will allow him to see the progress.

To be achieved team goals require a contribution from all team members. Just as with individual goals, there are team goals for each practice, each week, each month, each testing, each tournament, and each season. They are usually discussed and determined at team meetings. Team discussion and team decision increase both goal awareness and commitment. They produce a form of psychological contracting which binds the team to serious practice. Once set through the coach's assistance, team goals increase team unity and continuously exert strong social pressure upon all members to continue according to expectations since each member is an integral and necessary part of the whole.

Psychologists have suggested several guidelines that can be helpful in using goal-setting as a motivational tool.

(1) Goals should be *objective* and *specific* (improve speed-drill time by eight seconds, improve the vertical jump by two centimetres, etc) rather than general ('do your best,' 'try and improve by as much as you can,' etc.);

(2) Goals should be *meaningful* (the player's vertical jump compares well - at the top - to the norms of his age group, etc);

(3) Goals should be *obtainable* (realistic and yet demanding objectives - 50 % chance of achievement – are most effective goals for the player to strive for); and

(4) Goals should be *individualized* and should be based on past experience. The coach must know the athlete's abilities and limitations, as well as his aspiration levels. Only then can the coach formulate the athlete's realistic but challenging goals fairly accurately.

Final thought

It will be impossible for a coach to employ all of the motivational suggestions presented in this section. He or she may choose a few and build on them with ideas that may develop as he or she continues with his or her program. There are virtually no limits to the types of motivational ideas that can be developed and/or borrowed from other successful programs (not necessarily from soccer). However, every coach must also realize that no motivational procedure or strategy will have a lasting effect unless he or she knows how to teach correct soccer skills and strategies, how to apply contemporary training methods, and how to work with athletes.

Inspirational slogans

To increase his motivational effectiveness the coach may use inspirational words and phrases that will get his team focused and motivated. Slogans for the day, week, or a specific game can be a useful tool. A small selection of inspiring slogans taken from *The Great Book of Inspiring Quotations,* a Sport Books Publisher publication, has been compiled in the next section. The coach can select whichever suit his or her team best.

Character

After many years in which the world has afforded me many experiences, what I know most surely in the long run about morality and obligations, I owe to football (soccer).
ALBERT CAMUS

The greatest of faults, I should say, is to be conscious of none.
THOMAS CARLYLE

Character equals destiny.
HERACLITUS

A man may make mistakes, but he isn't a failure until he starts blaming someone else.
JOHN WOODEN

Try not to become a man of success, but rather try to become a man of value.
ALBERT EINSTEIN

In the arena of human life, the honours and rewards fall to those who show their good qualities in action.
ARISTOTLE

Waste no time arguing what a good man should be. Be one.
MARCUS AURELIUS ANTONINUS

Talent will get you to the top, but it takes character to keep you there.
JOHN WOODEN

Nobody holds a good opinion of a man who has a low opinion of himself.
ANTHONY TROLLOPE

Win without boasting, lose without excuse.
ALBERT PAYSON TERHUNE

There is never a better measure of what a person is than what he does when he is absolutely free to choose.
WILLIAM M. BULGER

A sound body is good; a sound mind is better; but a strong and clean character is better than either.
THEODORE ROOSEVELT

Hard work spotlights the character of people: some turn up their sleeves, some turn up their noses, and some don't turn up at all.
SAM EWIG

Character is what you know you are, not what others think you have.
MARVA COLLINS

Desire

We desire most what we ought not to have.
PUBLILIUS SYRUS

There couldn't be a society of people who didn't dream. They'd be dead in two weeks.
WILLIAM BURROUGHS

A champion must have the desire for perfection, and the will to punish himself in the process.
ANONYMOUS

Strength is not nearly as important as desire. I don't think you can teach anyone desire. I think it's a gift. I don't know why I have it, but I do.
LARRY BIRD

If one advances confidently in the direction of his dreams, and endeavours to live the life which he has imagined, he will meet with a success unexpected in common hours.
HENRY DAVID THOREAU

Desire! That's the one secret of every man's career. Not education. Not being born with hidden talents. Desire.
BOBBY UNSER

Man's desires are limited by his perceptions; none can desire what he has not perceiv'd.
WILLIAM BLAKE

We accomplish things by directing our desires, not ignoring them.
JOHN HENRY NEWMAN

The first principle of success is desire—knowing what you want. Desire is the planting of your seed.
ROBERT COLLIER

If you really want something, you can figure out how to make it happen.
CHER

If everyone got what they wanted, there wouldn't be enough to go around.
ANONYMOUS

If it is meant to be, it is up to me.
SHERRY BASSIN

Excellence

The only sin is mediocrity.
MARTHA GRAHAM

It isn't hard to be good from time to time in sports. What's tough is being good every day.
WILLIE MAYS

It takes a long time to bring excellence to maturity.
PUBLILIUS SYRUS

We are what we repeatedly do.... Excellence, then, is not an act but a habit.
ARISTOTLE

All things excellent are difficult, as they are rare.
BARUCH SPINOZA

The same man cannot well be skilled in everything; each has his special excellence.
EURIPEDES

I don't ask our athletes how many of them want to win. The question I ask is can you live with losing, can you live with failure, can you live with mediocrity?
LOU HOLTZ

In the pursuit of excellence, there is no finish line.
ROBERT H. FORMAN

The secret of joy in work is contained in one word—excellence. To know how to do something well is to enjoy it.
PEARL BUCK

I know it sounds selfish, wanting to do something no one else has done. But that's what you're out here for... to separate yourself from everyone else.
JACK NICKLAUS

With regard to excellence, it is not enough to know, but we must try to have and use it.
ARISTOTLE

Next year is not about winning another championship, or having one more ring, or developing bigger reputations. It's about leaving footprints.
PAT RILEY

Welcome the task that makes you go beyond yourself.
FRANK MCGEE

Focus

Nothing can add more power to your life than concentrating all of your energies on a limited set of targets.
NIDO QUBEIN

Those who attain to any excellence commonly spend life in some single pursuit, for excellence is not often gained upon easier terms.
SAMUEL JOHNSON

When every physical and mental resource is focused, one's power to solve a problem multiplies tremendously.
NORMAN VINCENT PEALE

Who begins too much accomplishes little.
GERMAN PROVERB

Yesterday is not ours to recover, but tomorrow is ours to win or lose.
LYNDON BAINES JOHNSON

Do not look back. And do not dream about the future, either. It will neither give you back the past, nor satisfy your other daydreams. Your duty, your reward – your destiny – are here and now.
DAG HAMMARSKJÖLD

You can destroy your now by worrying about tomorrow.
JANIS JOPLIN

Focus... is a process of diverting one's scattered forces into one powerful channel.
JAMES ALLEN

The only game you should think about winning is the next one.
ANONYMOUS

I believe when you are in any contest, you should work as though there is, to the very last minute, a chance to lose.
DWIGHT D. EISENHOWER

Concentrate... put all your eggs in one basket, and watch that basket....
ANDREW CARNEGIE

There is no job so simple that it cannot be done wrong.
ANONYMOUS

Goals

When I am working on a problem, I never think about beauty. I think only of how to solve the problem. But when I have finished, if the solution is not beautiful, I know it is wrong.
BUCKMINSTER FULLER

All my life I wanted to be somebody. Now I see that I should have been more specific.
JANE WAGNER

The direction of the mind is more important than its progress.
JOSEPH JOUBERT

If a man takes no thought about what is distant, he will find sorrow near at hand.
CONFUCIUS

We see obstacles when we take our eyes off our goals.
ANONYMOUS

If you would hit the mark, you must aim a little above it;
Every arrow that flies feels the attraction of earth.
HENRY WADSWORTH LONGFELLOW

A journey of a thousand miles must begin with a single step.
CHINESE PROVERB

Acting without thinking is like shooting without aiming.
B. C. FORBES

Be aware that the only ceiling life has is the one you give it.
ANONYMOUS

A man's worth is no greater than the worth of his ambitions.
MARCUS AURELIUS ANTONINUS

Who shoots at the midday sun, though he be sure he shall never hit the mark, yet as sure he is he shall shoot higher than who aims but at a bush.
SIR PHILIP SIDNEY

Planning is bringing the future into the present so that you can do something about it now.
ALAN LAKEIN

Visualize yourself as the player you want to be.
ANONYMOUS

Happiness

The only happy people I know are the ones who are working well at something they consider important.
ABRAHAM MASLOW

The more difficult a victory, the greater the happiness in winning.
PELE

Happiness depends upon ourselves.
ARISTOTLE

The happy man is not he who seems thus to others, but who seems thus to himself.
PUBLILIUS SYRUS

I can live for two months on a good compliment.
MARK TWAIN

Happiness is like coke – something you get as a by-product in the process of making something else.
ALDOUS HUXLEY

Happiness is having a scratch for every itch.
OGDEN NASH

Enjoy the little things, for one day you may look back and realize they were the big things.
ROBERT BRAULT

Pleasure is very seldom found where it is sought; our brightest blazes of gladness are commonly kindled by unexpected sparks.
SAMUEL JOHNSON

When one door of happiness closes, another opens; but often we look so long at the closed door that we do not see the one which has been opened for us.
HELEN KELLER

There is no duty we so much underrate as the duty of being happy.
ROBERT LOUIS STEVENSON

Happiness is loving what you do, even if you don't do it well.
GEORGE BURNS

Intelligence

A feeble mind weakens the body.
JEAN JACQUES ROUSSEAU

Better know nothing than half-know many things.
FRIEDRICH WILHELM NIETZSCHE

Nothing can be loved or hated unless it is first known.
LEONARDO DA VINCI

To do what others cannot do is talent. To do what talent cannot do is genius.
WILL HENRY

It is not enough to have a good mind. The main thing is to use it well.
RENÉ DESCARTES

Where all think alike, no one thinks very much.
WALTER LIPPMANN

The bold are helpless without cleverness.
EURIPEDES

Everything worth thinking has already been thought; our concern must only be to try to think it through again.
JOHANN WOLFGANG VON GOETHE

Not to know is bad; not to wish to know is worse.
NIGERIAN PROVERB

Activity is the only road to knowledge.
GEORGE BERNARD SHAW

The Lord gave us two ends; one for thinking, one for sitting. Heads you win, tails you lose.
ANONYMOUS

Intelligence is defined as the ability to adjust.
ANONYMOUS

Intelligence is content to point out the road, but never drives us along it.
ALEXIS CARREL

Learning

It is good to rub and polish your mind against the minds of others.
MICHEL EYQUEM DE MONTAIGNE

The beautiful thing about learning is nobody can take it away from you.
B. B. KING

Failure is the only opportunity to move intelligently to begin again.
HENRY FORD

Live as if you were to die tomorrow. Learn as if you were to live forever.
MAHATMA GANDHI

Learn from yesterday, live for today, hope for tomorrow.
ALBERT EINSTEIN

What matters is what I've done and what I'll leave behind. Let it be an example for those that come.
PELE

It is impossible for someone to learn about that which he thinks he knows.
EPICTETUS

The only real mistake is the one from which we learn nothing.
JOHN POWELL

I learned that good judgment comes from experience and that experience grows out of mistakes.
OMAR N. BRADLEY

Whenever you fall, pick up something.
OSWALD THEODORE AVERY

Experience is not what happens to a man. It is what a man does with what happens to him.
ALDOUS HUXLEY

Learn from the mistakes of others – you can never live long enough to make them all yourself.
ANONYMOUS

No coach has ever won a game by what he knows; it's what his players have learned.
ALONZO STAGG

PART III

LEAD-UP GAMES

The collection of lead-up games in this section includes mainly game types that have an immediate relationship to playing effective soccer. They are an important part of the general, as well as soccer-specific, practice because of their joyful and performance-stimulating character. They are a connecting link between necessary basic preparation and more soccer-specific training because they prepare, develop, and strengthen players' technical and tactical skills. As part of modern soccer training they should be used in a way that they are well balanced with other aspects of training.

Each lead-up game has a certain function to fulfill in physical, technical, or psychological respect. It should have a specific purpose and meet the objectives the coach has set for the practice. The following tips should be considered:

• Use lead-up games mainly as an introduction for new movements and techniques of the game. However, they can also serve as a relaxing part during the middle part of training and provide some counter balance to the more demanding soccer-specific drills and training elements. Lead-up games can be used as fun drills at the end of practice to end workout on a joyful note.

• Lead-up games should follow a progression, moving from the simple to more complex. Build up on previous experiences, and develop a progression of lead-up games for each skill taught.

• Know the game very well. Small organizational mistakes confuse the players and lower the value of practice. Well-planned lead-up games make practice enjoyable and increase players' motivation for further improvements.

• Explain the lead-up games clearly and demonstrate it before the players practice it. The explanation should be clear and concise making sure that every player has a clear understanding of the task.

• Equipment has to be ready to ensure a quick start of the game. This also applies to team markings, field markings, etc.

• Make sure that the lead-up games are executed correctly. After a clear explanation and demonstration, it's coach's responsibility to see that the lead-up game is done correctly. If the execution is sloppy or not correct, the practice must be stopped and the correct method emphasized one more time.

• As much as possible, introduce competition into lead-up games. This raises the intensity level of practice. Acknowledge the winner and praise good work.

• Check whether everything was done to give the selected lead-up game a joyful aspect.

Developing technical skills without the ball

Starting and stopping

Coaching note

Soccer is a game of stops and starts and quick, complex movements. Players will benefit from using these games as a lead-up to other training, without having to focus on the ball.

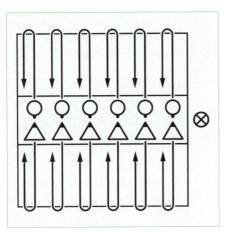

G1 Baseline race   Two groups of equal number stand facing each other in the centre of the playing area. When the signal is given, each group turns and runs to the baseline behind them and back. The first group to return to its original position receives a point. Starting positions (e.g., standing, sitting, lying face down, etc.) and mode of movement (e.g., running, skipping, hopping, etc.) can be varied. The team with the most points after several rounds is the winner.

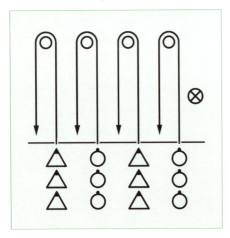

G2 Relay competition   Several groups of equal number line up in a row behind a designated start line with adequate separation between groups. Each group has a marker (e.g., cone or pylon) positioned several metres ahead of it. At the signal, the first member of each group runs up to and around the marker, returns to the baseline, and tags the next player in line, and so on. The first group to return to its original position wins. If numbers are uneven to start, one player can go twice.

G3 **Start tag** The players, and one player chosen to be IT, stand on opposite sides of a playing area divided into three equal parts. At the signal, all players try to successfully make it from one baseline to the other without being tagged by IT. Before tagging any players, IT must first run across a third of the playing area to pick up an object, such as a cone, to be used to tag other players. All players who are tagged must also pick up cones and help IT in subsequent rounds. The winner is the last player tagged.

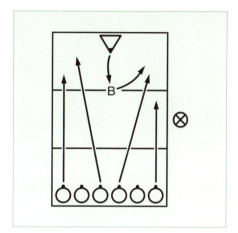

G4 **Black & white** Two teams of equal number stand facing each other a certain distance apart in the centre of the playing area. One team is called "black" and the other is called "white." At the signal of the coach ("black" or "white"), each member of that team must run to the baseline behind them as they are pursued by members of the opposing team. The goal of the other team is to tag as many players as possible before they reach the baseline safely. The team gets a point for each opposing player tagged. After repeating the game several times, the team tallying the most points is the winner.

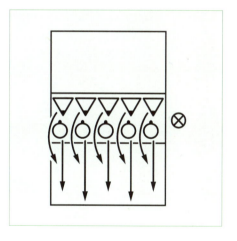

G5 **Position change** Two teams of equal number stand facing each other at opposite ends of a rectangular playing area. At the signal, both teams run to opposite sides. The first team to stand in a row along the opposite baseline wins.

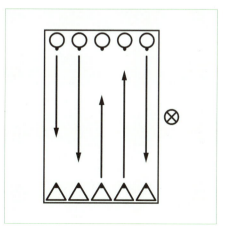

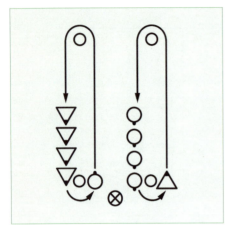

G6 **Chase** Two teams position themselves as shown. Each team assigns one player to be IT, who lines up next to the opposing team. At the signal, players begin circling around two pylons placed several metres apart. The player who is IT for each team must chase and try to tag the last player on the opposing team. Each team tries to prevent this as long as possible without losing their original order. The first team to successfully tag a player gains a point. New players are chosen to be IT for each round.

Turning

Coaching note

During a game players will "turn" for a variety of reasons: to attack; to elude; to shoot; to receive a pass; or to find space. One of the most used words on a soccer field is "turn!"— usually shouted by the passer of the ball towards the receiver of the ball.

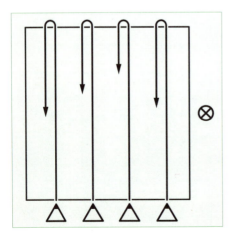

G7 **Save your soul** Players stand behind one baseline of a rectangular playing area. At the signal, all players run to the opposite baseline and back. The last player to return to the starting baseline after each round receives a point and starts one metre ahead of everyone else in the next round. The object is to finish the game with as few points as possible.

G8 ✓ **Accordion run** A rectangular playing area is divided into three equal parts marked by lines. Players start at one baseline and have to run to each line and back (i.e., to the first line and back, to the second line and back, and to the final line and back). This requires fast running and turning. The winner is the player with the most wins after several rounds.

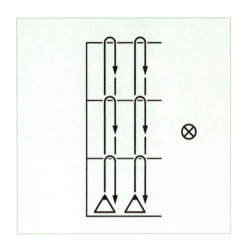

G9 ✓ **Row run** Teams of equal number stand in rows next to each other. All players are given a number. When the coach calls out a number, the player from each team with that number must run around his or her team in a counterclockwise direction before returning to his or her original position. The first player to return to his or her original position receives a point for the team. Different numbers are called out in each round until all players have run at least once. The team accumulating the most points wins.

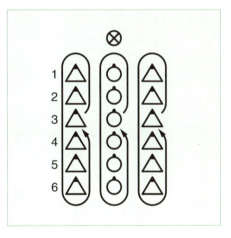

G10 **Circle tag** A small group (not more than 10 players) stands in a circle formation holding hands. A player chosen to be IT stands outside the circle and must try to tag a designated player from the circle. The circle tries to protect this player from being tagged by turning, but must do so without breaking the circle (i.e., releasing hands). When the player is successfully tagged, a different player becomes IT.

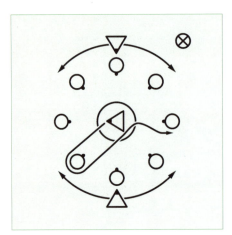

G11 <u>Circling</u> One group (not larger than 12 to 15 players) stands in a circle. One player stands in the middle of the circle and two others outside the circle. At the signal, the player in the middle tries to circle around one member of the circle without being tagged by one of the two players outside the circle. The player inside the circle must try to circle three different players. If the runner gets tagged, the tagger becomes a runner, or three new people are chosen.

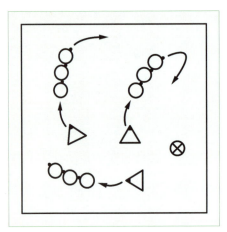

G12 <u>Attaching</u> In groups of three, each player stands holding the hips of the player in front of him or her (except the first player). One group of three is IT. Individually, the players who are IT try to get themselves attached to a group by grabbing the hips of the last player in line. The group tries to avoid this by turning. If a player manages to become attached, his or her team is no longer IT and the team that has not succeeded in turning well enough and has been captured, becomes the IT team.

Evading and faking

Coaching note

While evading and faking lead-up games can be used in a variety of sports, the skills are applied in soccer when "losing your marker" (evading) and "beating the defender" (faking). Tag games provide excellent simulations of soccer's attacker-defender interactions.

G13 **Traditional tag**   One player is chosen to be IT and must try tagging another player in the group within a bounded playing area. A tagged player then becomes IT. Touchbacks are not permitted.

G14 **Protection tag**   As above, except players can use certain positions agreed upon before the game (e.g., squat, piggyback with another player, hold hands with another player, stork stand, etc.) to avoid being tagged. Players are only "protected" for a limited period of time (up to five seconds) before IT can tag them again, but IT cannot guard protected players.

G15 **Cross tag**   A pursued player can be saved if another player runs between this player and IT, thus cutting the path between IT and the player. IT then is not allowed to continue pursuing the original player. However, he may attempt to tag the person crossing his or her path. If IT is successful, roles are reversed.

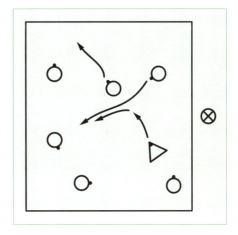

G16 **Chain tag**   One or more players are IT to begin the game. As players are tagged, they must join hands with IT, becoming part of a longer chain. The chain must remain connected at all times, so only the first and last players forming the chain are able to tag remaining players. The game continues until all players have been tagged.

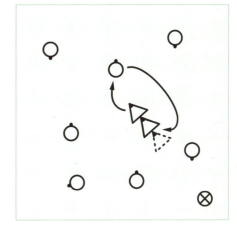

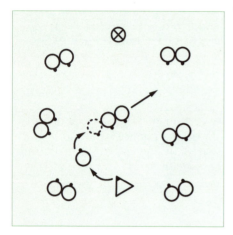

G17 <u>Tag the third</u> Players are paired (linked by the arms) and scattered throughout the playing area. Two players remain unpaired, one of whom begins the game IT. IT tries to tag the other unpaired player, who can save him- or herself by linking arms with one of the pairs. Only two players can be linked at one time, so when a third player links up with a pair, the outermost player must release and form a new pair while avoiding being tagged, and so on. If IT successfully tags another player before he or she is able to link up with another pair, that player becomes IT. No touchbacks are allowed.

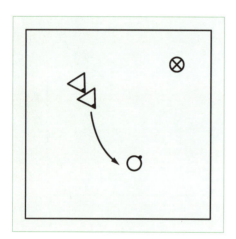

G18 <u>Two catch one</u> In a group of three, two players hold hands and try to tag the third player within a marked playing area. Whoever successfully tags the third player, without letting go of his or her partner's hand, switches roles with the tagged player.

G19 <u>Time tag</u> In a marked playing area, IT has to catch as many players as possible within a certain time limit (e.g., 30 seconds). *Variation:* IT has to tag everyone as fast as possible. Tagged players squat down and become obstacles for the remaining players. After each player has been IT once, the player who successfully tags everyone in the fastest time is declared the winner. For added difficulty, the number of players who are IT to start the game can be gradually increased.

G20 <u>Collecting pinnies</u> Everyone is IT in this game. All players tuck a pinnie into the back of their pants or shorts and must try to grab as many other players' pinnies as possible, while protecting their own. The player who successfully collects the most pinnies after a specified period of time is the winner.

G21 **Pair tag** All players form pairs by holding hands. One pair is IT. When the IT pair tag another pair, the tagged pair is IT.

Variations:

- Pair tag with held hands: as above, except the IT pair must tag other pairs with their joined hands.

- Pair tag with restriction: all players form pairs by holding hands. Only the player on one side of the pair can tag or be tagged, depending on the call of the coach or instructor: "left... right... left, etc."

- Gallop pair tag: similar to pair tag, except pairs must stand facing each other, hold both of their partner's hands, and travel by galloping. The pair designated IT must also move this way.

G22 **Relay tag** A group of players are chosen to be IT and sit or stand along the baseline of a square playing area. Another group of equal number moves around within the playing area. One at a time, each player who is IT has to run into the playing area and tag one player before being able to run back outside the playing area. When a player is successfully tagged and IT has left the playing area, the next player who is IT enters the playing area, must tag another player, and so on. The game is over when each tagger has tagged one player. Roles are later reversed.

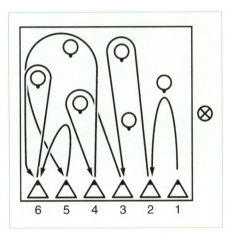

G23 **Three-team tag** Players form three equal teams. One team is IT and spreads out in a large playing area. The players from both other teams stand along a baseline and must try to run across the playing area to the opposite baseline and back without being tagged. The taggers try to tag as many players as possible. A player who has been tagged can reenter the game once he or she is back at the starting baseline. Each successful run in one direction is worth one point. After two minutes, the game is stopped and another group becomes IT. After each group is IT once, points are tallied to determine the winning team.

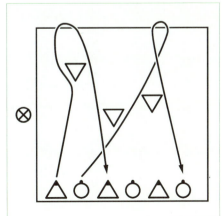

Jumping

G24 <u>Jumping over a distance</u> Players line up in a row behind a designated start line. At the signal, players have to cover a specified distance by jumping. The coach or instructor will determine whether or not it is left-footed, right-footed, or two-footed jumping, and how many times the players will be required to jump the required distance.

G25 <u>Grid jump fight</u> Players stand in pairs facing each other on one foot with arms crossed. One player stands in a small grid, marked by four cones, while the other jumps around the outside. Both have their arms crossed and try to get the other player to put both feet down. The player outside the grid also tries to push the other one outside the grid. Players switch positions after each round. The player winning the most rounds is the winner.

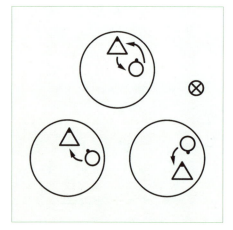

G26 <u>Rooster fight</u> Two players face each other in a fighting position (arms crossed in front, standing on one leg) and jump towards each other when the signal is given. Players try knocking each other off balance without unfolding their arms until one player is forced to put both feet on the ground. The game can be played in teams—the winning team would be the one with the most players still on one leg with arms crossed after a specified period of time. A circular fighting ring may also be used to make the game more difficult. Any player stepping out of the ring would be eliminated.

G27 Jump tag Two groups stand facing each other a few metres apart at one end of the playing area. One group is IT to start the game. At the signal, the players must begin jumping towards a goal line at the opposite end of the playing area. Players who are IT must try tagging as many of them as possible before they safely reach the goal. Groups switch roles after each round. Points are tallied after a few rounds to determine the winner. *Variations*: (a) players must jump on one foot; (b) players must jump on two feet; (c) players who are IT decide on the mode of jumping before each round begins.

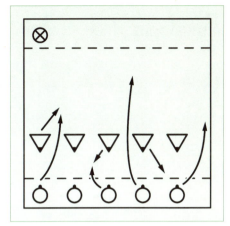

G28 Jumping over players Two groups each form a circle lying face down with their heads towards the centre. At the signal, the first player in each group gets up and jumps over the other players in a counterclockwise direction until returning to his or her original position. As soon as the first player has jumped over the person next to him or her, this player also gets up and begins jumping over the others in the same direction, and so on, until each player has jumped over every other player. The first team to have each member return to his or her original position is the winner.

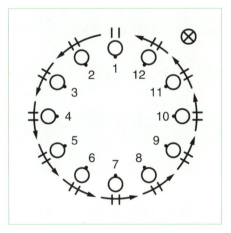

G29 Jumping over the rope The coach or another player stands in the middle of a circle formed by the remaining players. The player in the middle swings a rope with a sandbag (or similar object) attached to the end of it just above the ground in a clockwise direction, for five to ten revolutions. Players in the circle must jump over the rope as it passes them. If a player touches the rope at any time, he or she replaces the player in the middle; otherwise, players take turns as the middle player. *Variations*: (a) speed and height of the swing can be varied; (b) players move in the opposite direction of the swing.

Developing technical skills with the ball

Getting used to the ball

Coaching note

Every good warm-up should consist of getting players reacquainted with the ball. Simple drills that may not even be soccer-based can provide a good lead-up to more complex or demanding ball-based drills.

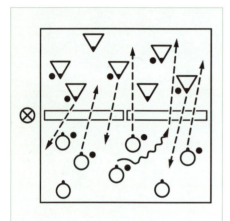

G30 **Balls be gone** Two teams stand facing each other on opposite sides of a playing area of any size divided equally by a row of cones (or benches). Each team starts with the same number of balls. At the signal, each team tries to get their balls into the opponent's half of the playing area as fast as possible. The balls can be thrown, kicked, or moved by any other means. The game is played for a specified time, or until all the balls are in one half of the playing area at one time. If playing for a limited time, the team with the fewest balls in their half wins.

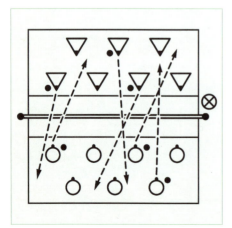

G31 **Multi-ball** Two teams stand on opposite sides of a playing area divided equally by a net or rope. The object of the game is to get as many balls as possible into the opposing team's half of the playing area in a given time. Any technique can be used to get the balls over the net, but players cannot cross over a line one metre away from the net on either side when doing so. Any player crossing over this line receives a minus point for the team. A ball must hit the floor within the boundaries on the opposing side to count as a point. Balls can be passed among team members as often as desired.

G32 **Ball retrieval race**   Two teams stand facing each other at opposite ends of the playing area, with several balls placed along the centre line. At the signal, both teams run to the middle to retrieve as many balls as possible and bring them back to their starting line. The team gathering the most balls is the winner. *Variation*: the coach could chose a progression of skills: set 1— carrying the ball back by hand; set 2— dribbling the ball back by feet; set 3— juggling the ball all the way back in the air.

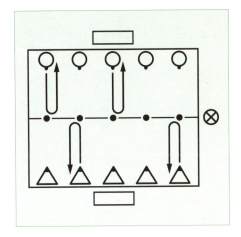

Dribbling

Coaching note

Whether we are dealing with children or professionals, there can never be enough dribbling drills in the coach's repertoire. Dribbling is one of the key skills in soccer, as it allows for both control of the ball and attacking soccer. To dribble well, is to control the game.

G33 **Circle dribbling**   Players form two or more groups of equal number and stand in a large circle (marked by cones) with some separation between groups. The first player in each group is given a ball and dribbles around the circle in a counterclockwise direction. When he or she has completed the full circle, the ball is passed off to the next player in line and he or she joins the end of the line. This continues until the first player reaches the front of the line again. The drill is then repeated in a clockwise direction.

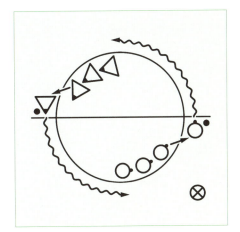

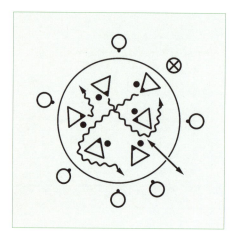

G34 <u>Autodrome</u> Players are divided into two groups. Each member of one group is given a ball and dribbles within a confined circular playing area for one minute. Players must continue moving and dribbling within the circle at a brisk pace determined by the coach, trying not to bump into other players, step out of bounds, or lose control of the ball. The next group then repeats the drill. Players from each team lasting the full minute without a fault then play one more round to determine a winner. In the final round, players actively try to knock the balls away from each other while dribbling. The last remaining player wins.

G35 <u>Circular track dribbling</u> Members of one team are each given a ball and dribble along a circular path (one to three metres wide). Another team of equal number stands around the circle watching for mistakes. The ball must remain within the circular path, and all players must remain in single file while moving around the circle. The objective for each team is to complete a specific number of revolutions around the circle as fast as possible. Mistakes result in extra seconds being added to a team's time (i.e., one mistake = five extra seconds). The team completing the rounds in the fastest time wins.

G36 <u>Dribble chase</u> Players are divided into equal teams and form a large circle, standing in alternating order facing the centre. Each player from every team is given a number (e.g., from one to four for teams of four players). When the coach or instructor calls out a number, all players with that number must dribble around the outside of the circle in the same direction and try to tag the person in front of them. The winner of each round is the first player to successfully tag the player ahead of him or her, or the first player to make it back to his or her position in the circle, while maintaining control of the ball.

G37 **Pendulum dribbling** Two teams of equal number are each divided in half, each half lined up facing the other from a given distance. The first player from each team is given a ball and, at the signal, dribbles over to the first player in line across from them, passes the ball off to this player, joins the back of the line, and so on. The first team to completely switch sides is the winner.

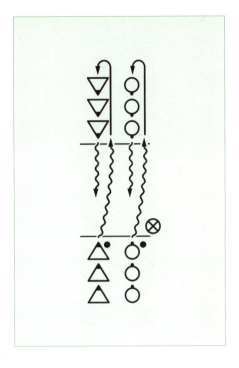

G38 **Turn dribbling** Players line up in a row one behind the other. The first player in line is given a ball and dribbles up to and around one or more cones before dribbling back, passing the ball off to the next player in line, and joining the back of the line. This game can be played with several teams as a relay— the first team to have the first player return to the front of the line is the winner.

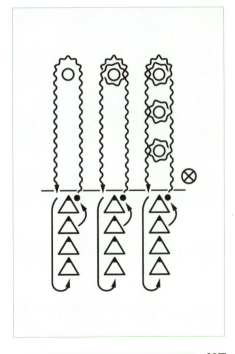

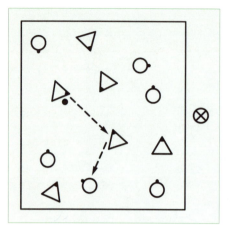

G39a **Hunter ball**   Two equal teams spread out in a large playing area. One team of players are hunters (and wear a pinnie) and the others are rabbits. When the coach throws the ball into play, a hunter picks up the ball and tries to hit a rabbit. The ball can be passed among hunters before shooting at the rabbits. Hunters receive a point each time a rabbit is hit. The same rabbit cannot be hit twice in a row. Rabbits receive a point if they catch a ball thrown at them or if a pass is dropped by the hunters. The team with the most points after a specified period of time is the winner. Teams then switch roles.

G39b **Rabbit ball**   A few players ("hunters") are chosen to be IT and are each given a ball. The remaining players are "rabbits." When the coach gives the signal, all the rabbits stand up and begin running around the playing area. Each hunter is given only one shot to tag a rabbit with the ball. Hunters successfully tagging a rabbit move on to the next round. Players who miss, switch roles with the rabbit in the following round. This is considered a dribbling game since players must move about (dribble) with the ball to get into perfect shooting position.

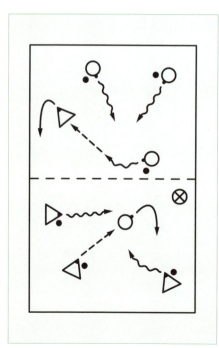

G39c **Fox ball**   In a large playing area, several "hunters" each have a ball and move around trying to tag the "fox." When the fox is tagged with the ball, the successful hunter becomes the fox. The goal for each player is to be the fox as often as possible and to successfully elude the hunter for as many rounds as possible. *Variation*: this game can also be played in teams, with the fox running around in the playing area of the opposing team. The team that hits the opposing fox first wins that round. The game continues until everyone has had a chance to be a fox at least once, and victories are tallied to determine a winner.

Touch drills

Coaching note

Although the need to have a good feel for the ball is important in many sports, soccer is different in that the ball is often redistributed immediately upon contact with a player's body. This is known as "one touch" soccer. As a result, the use of walls or tennis/net scenarios is a productive way to lead up to more pure soccer drills.

G40 **High ball**   Several teams are positioned on opposite sides of a playing area as shown in the diagram. The goal is to pass the ball over the net without letting the ball hit the ground, go out of bounds, or touch the net. The team that successfully passes the ball longest is the winner. *Variations*: (a) a maximum of three touches is permitted per side before the ball must be sent back over to the other side; (b) the game can also be played without a net. In this case, the goal is to pass the ball beyond a designated line on each side of the playing area.

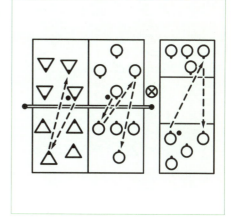

G41 **Volley challenge**   Two groups of equal number line up facing each other on opposite sides of a playing area separated by a neutral zone. Each player is matched up with another player on the other side of the neutral zone. One player feeds the ball to the other ten times and the ball is played (volleyed with the instep) back to the feeder. The ball must completely clear the neutral zone when returned to the feeder. After ten successful passes, roles are reversed. *Variations*: (a) feeders rotate one position to the right after each feed; (b) the size of the neutral zone is increased after each successful series of passes.

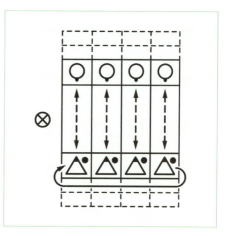

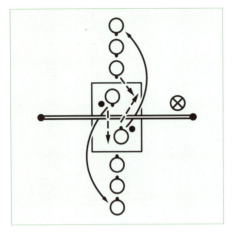

G42 <u>Pass-and-run tennis</u> Two teams stand in a row facing each other on opposite sides of a net. The first player on one team begins the drill by passing the ball over the net to the first player on the other team. After playing the ball over the net, each player must run under the net to join the end of the row on the other side. The drill continues until someone commits an error, which results in a point for that player. Errors include not getting the ball over the net, passing the ball out of bounds, or allowing the ball to touch the ground. Players receiving three points are out of the game. The last remaining player wins.

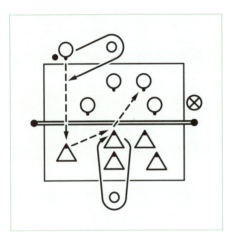

G43 <u>Soccer tennis</u> Two teams stand on opposite sides of a net. The ball is played back and forth, and can only bounce once before being played to a teammate or back over the net. The first team to reach 15 points wins the set. An error results in a point when the ball touches the net, goes out of bounds, bounces more than once, or is played more than three times by one team. Players rotate one position clockwise after each point and the ball goes to the team that lost the previous point. *Variation*: after each successful pass over the net, players must run around a cone on the baseline before rejoining the play.

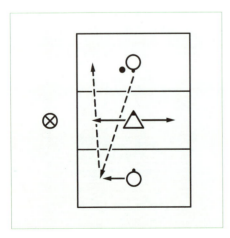

G44 <u>Monkey in the middle</u> A playing area is divided into three equal sections, with one player occupying each section. The two outermost players pass the ball to each other, trying to keep it out of the reach of the player in the middle (the monkey). After a passing error (the ball does not land in the correct section of the playing area or the ball is intercepted by the monkey), the player who committed the error becomes the new monkey. The winner is the player with the least number of errors after a given amount of time.

G45 **Double circle passing game**   Two circles are marked on the floor as shown in the diagram. All but three players stand outside the outer circle, with one player inside the inner circle, and two other players in the area between the two circles. A ball is passed back and forth between the player inside the inner circle and the players outside the outer circle. The two players between the circles must try to intercept the ball. If the ball is blocked or knocked away by one of these two players, the player switches positions with the unsuccessful passer.

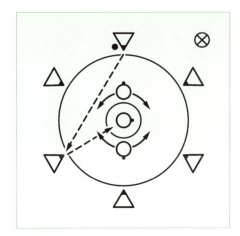

Shooting

Coaching note

Shooting is one of the most prized skills and requires countless repetitions for mastery. Lead-up games that prepare for more challenging or game-like drills are valid and indeed useful not only for warm-up, but also to engage the shooting mind in a different manner.

G46 **Rebound passing**   Players are divided into two or more equal groups. A series of lines are drawn parallel to a large, smooth wall at various distances from the wall. Each team lines up in a row (one behind the other) facing the wall behind the first line. Each player kicks the ball against the wall so it rebounds back past the start line. For each successful kick, the team receives a point. After each player has gone once, the starting distance from the wall is increased. The team with the most points after a certain number of rounds is the winner.

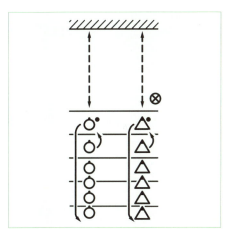

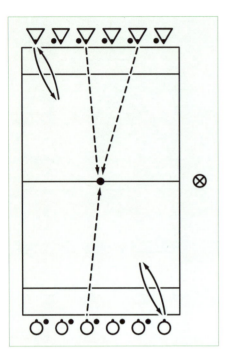

G47 Target ball   Two teams of equal number position themselves behind opposite baselines of a large playing area. An equal number of balls are given to each team to start the game. At the signal, the teams try to hit a larger ball lying in the centre of the playing area into the opponent's half of the playing area. Players can retrieve any balls lying in their half of the playing area, but must return to the baseline with the ball before attempting another shot. After a specified period of time, the team that successfully pushes the larger ball into the opposing team's half of the playing area is the winner. If the larger ball crosses a line one metre away from either baseline before the time is up, the ball is return to the centre and players return to their starting positions for the next round.

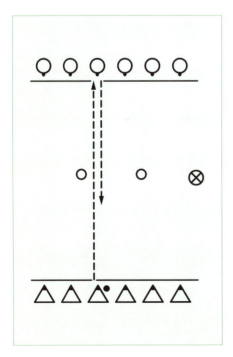

G48 Small-goal target game   Players are divided into two groups and stand on opposite sides of the playing area. A goal one metre wide is marked with cones in the centre of the playing area and players must try to kick a ball through the goal for a point. The player with the highest score after a specified amount of time is the winner.

G49 **Shooter vs. goalkeeper**   Players form groups of two. One player starts the game as the shooter and the other as the goalkeeper. When the shooter does not get his or her shot on goal, or the goalkeeper saves the shot, they switch roles. The first player to reach a certain number of goals is the winner.

G50 **Shooting through the line**   Two teams stand facing each other on opposite baselines a given distance apart. The ends of each baseline are marked with cones as goals and the players line up in a row along the baseline defending the goal. Each team begins the game with one ball. At the signal, each team tries to kick their ball into the opponent's goal. The ball must remain below head height to be a valid goal. Blocked shots and free balls can be retrieved by any player, but shots can only be taken from the baseline. The game continues until a total of ten goals are scored.

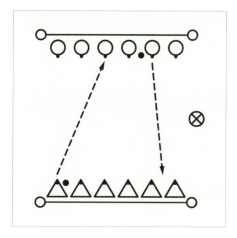

G51 **Drop kick shooting gallery**   Two teams of equal number stand facing each other at opposite ends of the playing area divided by a centre line. Neither team can pass this line during the game. Half of each team defends a goal in their end, and the other half tries to score on the opposing team. Each team receives a point by either hitting one of the offensive players on the opposing team with the ball or shooting the ball into the opposing goal with a drop kick (a drop kick is when the ball is dropped from the hands and the foot makes contact with the ball immediately on the bounce). After a point is scored, roles are switched on each team. Only offensive players are permitted to drop kick the ball for a point, and only defensive players are allowed to catch balls that come towards them. The first team to accumulate ten points is the winner.

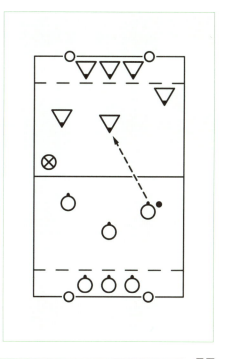

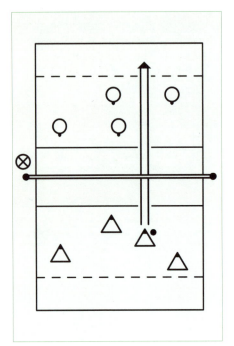

G52 **Ball under the rope**   Two teams of equal number stand on opposite sides of a playing area divided by a one-metre high rope. Players must try to kick the ball past the opponent's baseline for a point, keeping the ball below the height of the rope. A line one metre away from each side of the net cannot be crossed by either team before attempting a shot. Any errors (ball goes over the rope, ball touches the rope, player steps over the one-metre shooting line) also result in a point for the opposing team. The team with the most points after a certain amount of time is the winner. *Variation*: as above, except balls must be shot above the height of the rope. An actual net may be used instead of designating the baseline as the goal.

G53 **Head ball**   Players are divided into two equal teams. Goals can only be scored by playing the ball with the head. The ball can be kicked up and headed by the same player or headed off another player's kick. The game continues until a certain number of goals have been scored, or after a specific amount of time has elapsed.

Developing technical and tactical skills under pressure

Dribbling under pressure

> ## Coaching note
>
> *Players need to be able to dribble effectively under pressure. Such dribbling not only involves a player maintaining possession of the ball, but also being able to keep his or her head up in order to advance his or her position on the field, or make the best possible pass with clear vision. A dribbling lead-up game, with pressure, sets the stage for the kind of dribbling that will occur in more elaborate drills.*

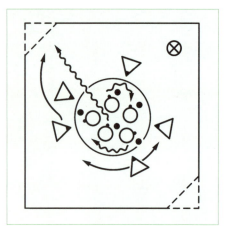

G54 <u>Dribbling to safety</u> Players are divided into dribblers and non-dribblers. Dribblers stand inside a circle in the centre of the playing area and non-dribblers stand outside the circle as defenders. Defenders cannot enter the circle at any time. The goal of the dribblers is to dribble to one of two safe zones in opposite corners without being touched by their non-dribbling partner. Everyone must be a dribbler once. The winner is determined through elimination.

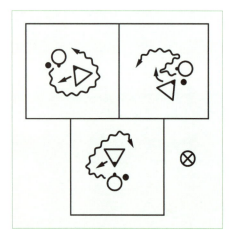

G55 <u>Dribble duel</u> Players are divided into pairs and stand within a small playing area. One player begins with the ball and dribbles within the boundaries of the playing area trying to maintain control and possession of the ball. The opposing player must try to steal the ball or knock it away from the ball carrier. The defending player receives a point each time the ball is stolen or knocked away. After one to two minutes the players switch roles. The player with the most points after several rounds is the winner.

G56 **<u>Number dribbling</u>** Players are divided into pairs. Each player is given a ball and dribbles in a large circular playing area. Each pair is also given a number, and each member of the pair is given one of two colours. One colour (blue) represents offense and the other (red) represents defense. When the coach calls out a number and a colour, the corresponding pair must react. The offensive player must dribble towards a goal and attempt a shot within the penalty area and the defensive player must leave his or her ball behind and try to take the ball away from the offensive player and defend the goal. Each successful play (a goal for the offensive player, no goal for the defensive player) earns a point. The player with the most points after several rounds is the winner.

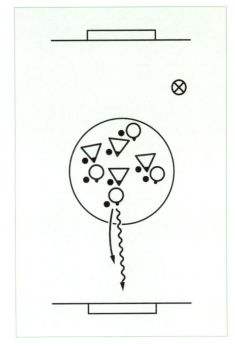

G57 **<u>Zone-to-zone dribbling</u>** A rectangular playing area with six equal sections is marked as shown. Players are divided into two equal teams. The members of one team are each given a ball and stand along one baseline. The members of the opposing team stand in alternate sections of the playing area as defenders. At the signal, players along the baseline must try to dribble to the opposite baseline without losing their balls. Dribbling players face one less defender in each successive section. Players who successfully make it across the playing area earn a point for the team. Players losing their ball must wait until the next round before rejoining the game. After a few rounds the teams switch roles. The team with the most points wins.

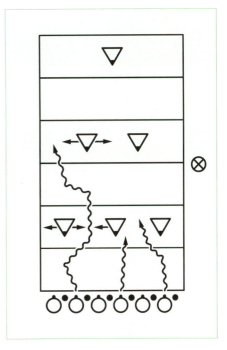

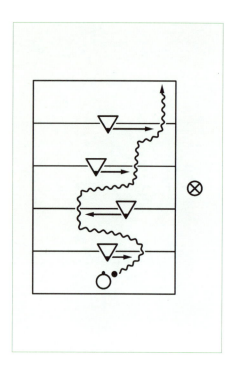

G58 <u>Dribbling against a row</u> A rectangular playing area is divided into as many equal sections as there are players (up to eight) as shown in the diagram. One attacking player stands on the baseline with a ball, and the remaining players each occupy one section of the playing area. The attacking player must try dribbling past each line of defense before reaching the opposite baseline. When the attacker reaches the opposite baseline, he or she becomes the last defender, and the first defender in the last round becomes the offensive player in the following round, and so on. The player who accumulates the most points (or makes the fewest mistakes) after several rounds is the winner.

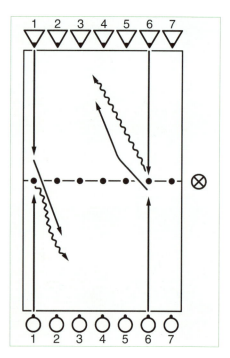

G59 <u>Ball battle dribble</u> Two teams of equal number stand directly opposite each other on opposite baselines of the playing area. Players on each team are given a number and stand in sequential order according to their assigned numbers. Several balls, equal to the number of players on each team, are placed along the centre line of the playing area (one ball per opposing pair). When the coach calls out a number, the players from each team with that number must run to the centre, and the first player to retrieve the ball must try dribbling back to his or her own baseline as quickly as possible. The opposing player must try to prevent him or her from successfully reaching the baseline with the ball. A point is awarded for each ball returned to the baseline. After a few rounds, the points for each team are compared to determine a winner. *Variation*: the coach calls out more than one number at a time.

G60 **Small-goal 1v1** In the middle of a square playing area, a two-metre-wide goal is marked with cones and a circular shooting line is drawn around the goal as shown. Two players alternate playing offense and defense. At the signal, the offensive player tries to score past the defender without crossing the shooting line. After a goal, a missed shot, or a change of possession, the players switch roles. After a certain amount of time has passed, the player with the most goals is the winner.

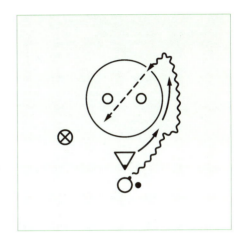

Passing under pressure

Coaching note

Passing under pressure requires a number of skills: protecting the ball; having good vision of the field and how the play is developing; precise delivery of the ball to a team-mate; and subsequent movement into open space to support the new ball possessor

G61 **Snap ball** In a large playing area, several groups play a passing game of "keep away" against "disturbers" in the following suggested ratios: 4:1, 6:2, 8:3. To create situations where players are more challenged to lose their men or mark their men, the following ratios are suggested: 3:1, 4:2, 2:1, 3:2, 4:3. In all these games, the disturbers try to steal or deflect the ball away from opposing players. When successful, the player who caused the mistake switches with the player who is judged to have made the mistake. Mistakes include the ball going out of bounds or being played too high.

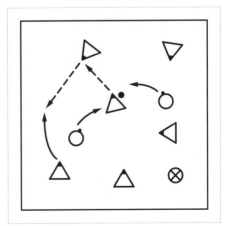

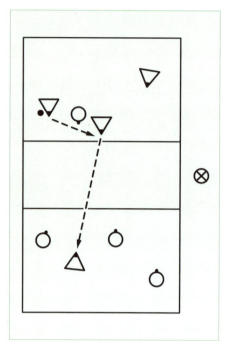

G62 **Target player**   Two teams of equal number, wearing different colours, stand facing each other on opposite sides of a playing area. The playing area is divided by a middle section that cannot be entered by any player during the game. Each team sends one player into the opponent's section of the playing area. The team with the ball must try to pass the ball to their teammate in the opponent's section of the playing area without entering the middle section or going out of bounds. A successful pass earns a point for the team. If the opposing team intercepts the ball, two new players are selected to play in the opponent's section. If a rule is broken (a player steps into the middle section, the ball goes out of bounds), the last player to touch the ball before the infraction gains possession of the ball. The team with the most points after a certain period of time is the winner.

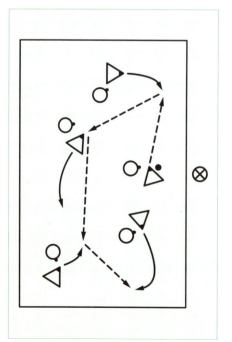

G63 **Possession**   Two teams of equal number, wearing different coloured shirts, stand in a large playing area. At the signal, the team with the ball must pass the ball among themselves to earn points. The coach will ensure that players in possession continuously move in support of one another. The opposing team must try to intercept the ball to earn points. The first team to reach 20 points, or the team that successfully passes the ball to five different teammates in succession, is the winner.

G64 **Possession with a neutral player**   In a large playing area, players are divided into two equal teams, with one neutral player assigned to switch to the other team when possession of the ball is lost. One team starts with the ball and must pass it among themselves without losing possession to the opposing team or losing the ball out of bounds. The team with the highest number of passes within a certain time limit is the winner.

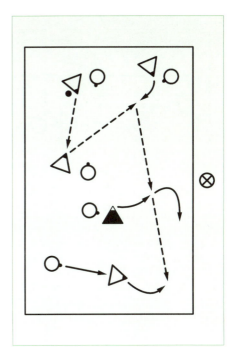

G65 **Sequential possession**   Players are numbered and must pass the ball in sequential order (player 1 to player 2, to player 3, etc.), without losing possession of the ball to the opposing team. The team earns a point when they successfully complete a series of passes. The ball changes hands after each series. The first team to reach a specified number of points, or the team with the most points after a specified time, is the winner.

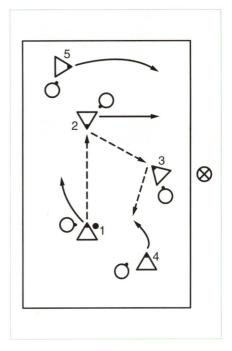

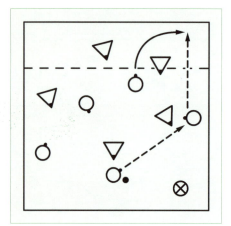

G66 <u>Baseline possession</u> Players are divided into two teams of equal number. The team starting with the ball must pass among themselves before eventually trying to pass the ball to a player as he or she enters the opponent's end zone. A player can only enter the end zone when he or she is expecting a pass, and must receive the pass completely within the boundaries of the end zone to earn a point. The first team to reach a certain number of points is the winner.

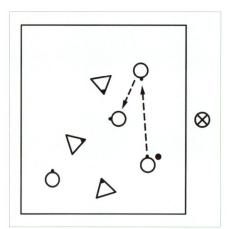

G67 <u>Outnumbered possession</u> Two teams are formed, one team outnumbering the other by one or more players. At the signal, the coach throws the ball into the playing area and the team that gains possession of the ball must try to keep possession as long as possible. A point is earned for every ten seconds the teams are able to keep the ball away from the opposing team, without allowing the ball to go out of bounds. Teams are rearranged every five minutes until everyone has been part of the outnumbered team at least once.

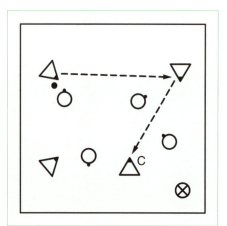

G68 <u>Captain ball</u> Two teams of equal number stand in a large playing area. Each team selects one player to be their captain. The team that be-gins the game with the ball must try to pass to their captain. Every time the captain successfully receives a pass, the team earns a point. The cap-tain cannot receive a pass from the same player twice in a row. After a certain amount of time, new captains are chosen for each team. The win-ner for each round is the team that accumulates the most points.

G69 **Possession and one pass**   A large
playing area is divided in half. Players are divided
into two teams, with half of each team standing
in each half of the playing area. At the signal, the
ball must be passed among team members (three
to eight times) without losing possession to the
opposing team, crossing over the centre line, or
losing the ball out of bounds. At least one pass in
the series must be to a teammate in the opposite
half of the playing area. When a team loses
possession of the ball before a series of passes is
completed, no points are awarded. One
successful series of passes earns one point for the
team. After each successful series of passes, the
opposing team gains possession of the ball. The
first team to reach a certain number of points, or
the team with the most points after a certain
amount of time, is the winner.

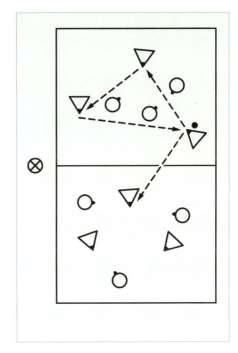

G70 **Passing for goals**   Two teams of equal
number stand in a large playing area with four to
six goals positioned randomly throughout the
playing area. At the signal, the coach or
instructor throws the ball into play and each
team must try to score a goal by passing the ball
through a goal to a teammate to earn one point.
The ball cannot be passed through the same goal
twice in a row. Before the ball can be passed
through another goal for a point, it must first be
touched by another player. Shots on goal can
come from either side of the goal. The team with
the highest score after a certain amount of time is
the winner.

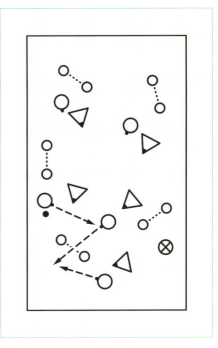

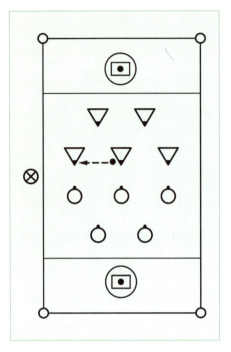

G71 Tower ball Two teams of equal number set up in a large playing area. At the signal, the team with the ball must pass the ball among themselves, and eventually to the tower guard (a teammate standing on a box) behind the opponent's line of defense, to earn a point. The tower guard must catch the ball or the point does not count. The opposing team gets the ball after each attempted pass or after a point is scored. The first team to reach a certain number of points is the winner.

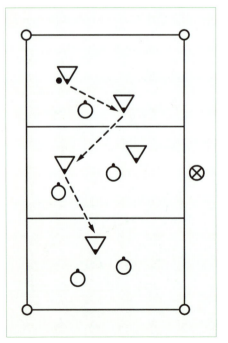

G72 Three-zone passing game A large playing area is divided into three equal parts. Two players from each team stand in the middle zone of the playing area, and two defensive players (from one team) and one offensive player (from the opposing team) stand in each end zone. One team starts with the ball from their own end zone, trying to pass the ball to a teammate in the middle zone, before eventually trying to pass the ball to their lone teammate in the opponent's end zone for a point. This is a very fast game, so players should be rotated frequently. The team with the highest score after a certain period of time is the winner.

Shooting under pressure

Coaching note

While shooting development requires considerable repetitions, it requires much more than that. Shooting is more than a basic skill—it is an instinct and a state of mind. Therefore, in order to develop shooters, the coach has to create game-like situations that not only consist of the presence of opponents, but also a visual challenge that inspires the shooting mind. Good shooting-based lead-up games can activate the shooting mind.

G73 Barbarians at the gate Players are divided into two equal teams. The offensive team starts with the ball and stands outside a half circle boundary marking the penalty area. The defensive players stand inside the penalty area guarding a goal positioned along the length of the baseline. Offensive players cannot touch or enter this area. Offensive players pass the ball among themselves before attempting a shot on goal, while the defenders try to prevent them from scoring. After 20 attempted shots on goal, the teams switch roles. The team with the most goals is the winner.

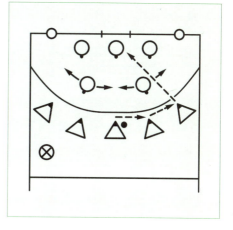

G74 Perimeter shooting vs. a shot-blocker Players are divided into pairs and position themselves as shown. One pair starts on offense and the other on defense. The offensive pair stands outside a half circle boundary marking the penalty area. The defensive pair stands inside the penalty area, one defending a goal positioned along the baseline, the other moving within a narrow path along the border of the penalty area. Offensive players may pass the ball to each other before attempting a shot, but must remain outside the penalty area at all times. After a specified time, the teams switch roles.

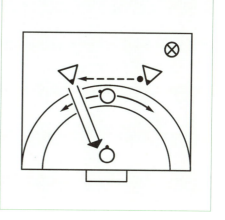

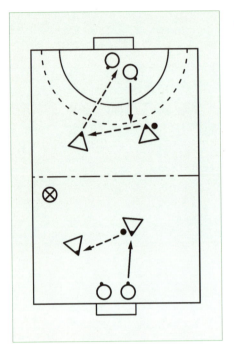

G75 __2v2 shooting__ Players are divided into pairs and position themselves as shown. One pair begins the game on offense and the other on defense. The offensive pair pass the ball around to each other and try to score into a goal positioned on the baseline of the playing area. The goalkeeper can leave the goal to block a shot or clear a loose ball. The game can be played with or without a penalty area boundary. After ten shots on goal, the teams switch roles. The team with the most goals wins.

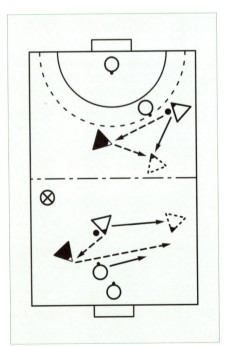

G76 __The playmaker__ Players are divided into offensive and defensive pairs and stand at one end of a playing area. The two offensive players try to score against two defenders. One player in the offensive pair plays the role of playmaker– able to pass and move, but not permitted to shoot on goal. After a certain period of time (three to five minutes), players switch roles. After each player has played the playmaker role at least once, the team with the most goals is the winner

G77 **Shoot and save** Players position themselves as shown. Four offensive players stand facing the goalkeeper from a given distance. At the signal, the first player challenges the goalkeeper one-on-one. After each shot, the offensive player becomes the goalkeeper and the goalkeeper joins the end of the line to become an offensive player. When each player has had at least five shots on goal, the player with the most goals is the winner.

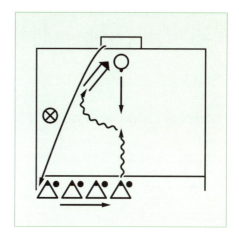

G78 **Wing shot scramble** Two offensive players play against a defender and a goalkeeper. The goalkeeper and defender start along the goal line, while the offensive players remain a certain distance from goal. The game begins with a shot on goal from the wing, which signals the defensive player to leave the goal line. The attackers try to score either on the initial shot or on a loose ball. The defender tries to either take control of the ball, block a second shot, or assist the goalkeeper. After each dead ball, players return to their original positions and start again. After ten shot attempts, players switch roles.

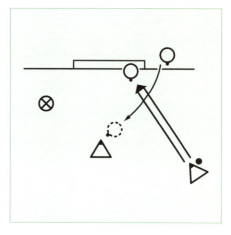

Developing advanced playing ability

Games using one goal

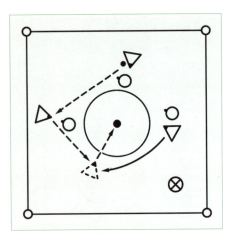

G79 <u>**Hit the big ball**</u>   A medicine ball is placed in the centre of a circle marked in the middle of a large playing area. At the signal, the coach throws a ball into the playing area. Two teams of three try to gain possession of the ball and hit the heavy ball in the centre without entering the circle. The ball may be passed among team members before attempting a shot. Each successful hit earns a point for the team. The team with the highest score after a certain period of time is the winner.

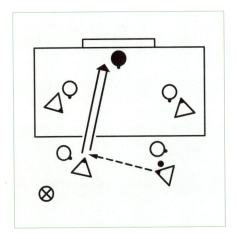

G80 <u>**Around the goal**</u>   Two teams of four stand in front of a goal in a large playing area. The goal is guarded by a neutral player. Each team tries to score a goal and to prevent the other team from doing the same. The first team to accumulate a certain number of points is the winner.

G81 <u>One-on-one</u> Players are divided into groups of three. Two players play a game of one-on-one, with the third player guarding a small goal. Two points are awarded for a goal, one point for a shot on goal. When a goal is scored or a shot is taken on goal, the shooter switches roles with the goalkeeper. The player with the most points after a certain amount of time wins.

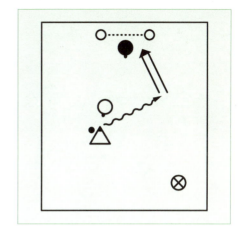

G82 <u>Two-on-two</u> As above, except players are divided into three pairs and play two-on-two with one goal. Each pair is given a particular number of attempts at goal before the goalkeepers are changed. The third pair rotates in goal for every attack. Every team must play against every other team at least once.

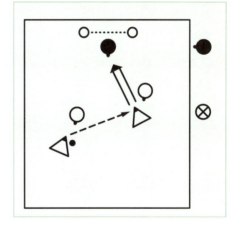

G83 <u>Two-on-one</u> Only two pairs are required per group. The coach sets a particular number of repetitions per group (e.g., ten). The attacking team will get a particular number of attempts at a goal defended by one player and count their goals. The defending team will rotate in goal after every attacking attempt. The defending team will become the attacking team after the set number of repetitions have been completed.

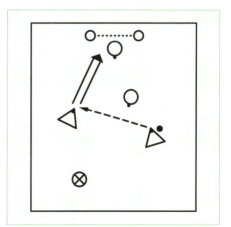

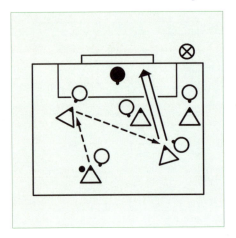

G84 <u>Penalty area possession</u> Players are divided into two equal teams. A neutral player is chosen to play in goal. After the coach throws the ball into play, the team that gains possession of the ball must try to score on goal, but must pass the ball at least once before attempting a shot. If a shot does not go into the net and the opposing team gets the rebound, the ball must be taken back outside the penalty area before being played on net again. If the same team that shot the ball gets the rebound, another shot can be attempted immediately. The team that scores retains possession of the ball.

Games using two goals

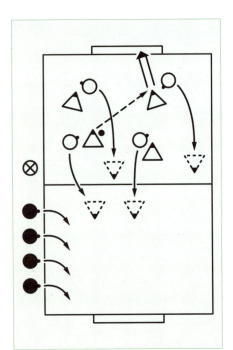

G85 <u>Pendulum game with three teams</u>
This game can be played on half a soccer field, using either small goals without goalkeepers, or regulation-sized portable goals with goalkeepers. Players are divided into three teams. One team begins the game on offense, one team on defense, and the other team sits off. Starting at one end of the field, the offense tries to score on the defense. When the offense scores or the defense gains possession of the ball, the defense goes on offense towards the goal at the other end of the field, the offense sits off, and the team that was sitting off becomes the new defending team. This pattern continues for a specified period of time. The team that scores the most goals in the allotted time is the winner.

G86 **Line game**   Two teams of equal number stand facing each other at opposite ends of a large playing area. Half of the players from each team are chosen to play in goal and the other half play offense and defense within the playing area. The goal for each team extends the entire width of the baseline at each end of the playing area with a three-metre crease extending outwards from each baseline. Goalkeepers are not allowed to leave the crease and no other players are allowed to enter the crease. If a player crosses this boundary, the opposing team is given a penalty shot a given distance from the goal. After a specified period of time, the team with the most goals is the winner. Players can switch roles halfway through the game.

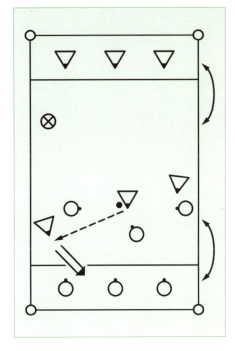

G87 **Score and switch sides**   Two small teams of equal number stand facing each other on opposite sides of a playing area with a goal at each end. Without a goalie tending either net, both teams try to score as many goals as possible on the opposing goal. A goal can only be scored when all the players on one team are in the opponent's half of the playing area. If a team scores a goal, they keep the ball and attack the goal at the other end of the playing area. The team that scores the most goals in the allotted time is the winner.

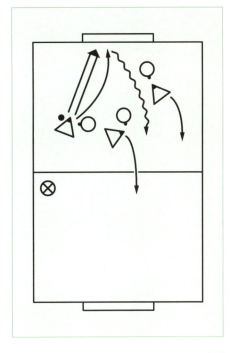

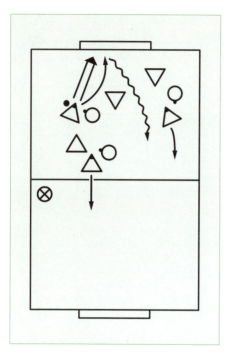

G88 Three-team score and switch Three teams play with two goals. Every time a team scores or gains possession, the team must attack the goal currently not in use.

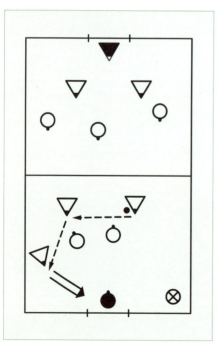

G89 Two-field game A large playing area with a goal at each end is divided in half by a centre line. Players are divided into two equal teams. Half of the players on each team occupy each half of the playing area. One half of the playing area is the offensive zone for one team and the defensive zone for the opposing team. One defender must play in goal for each team, creating an odd-man situation for the defense on each side. Players cannot cross the centre line at any time during the game – only the ball may cross the line. After a goal is scored, players on each team can switch positions. The first team to score ten goals is the winner.

G90 **Side-by-side small-goal shooting**

Players are divided into two equal teams and stand at opposite ends of a playing area. Several goals positioned along each baseline are each defended by one player. The remaining players on each team try to score on the opposing team and prevent the opposing team from doing the same. After a certain amount of time, the players on each team switch positions. The team that scores the most goals in the allotted time is the winner.

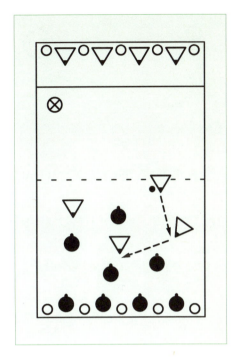

PART IV

DRILLS

'How you practice is how you play!' is well known saying in coaching. Effective, well-run drills at game-like intensity levels are the essence of training and a key ingredient in today's coaching. How the athletes relate to the coach is in many ways directly related to how the drills and practices are implemented.

This section presents over 130 game-specific drills divided into six main sections which aim to develop player's technical, tactical, and competition skills and abilities. The following guidelines should be considered when implementing drills into the training program:

• Drills should be applicable to the skills used in the game.

• Drills should challenge the skill level of the players.

• Drills should be varied. The coach should choose from a number of different drills that accomplish the same purpose. Include a fun drill in most practices.

• Generally, drills should be carried out at a tempo that simulates the action of the game. Practices conducted at high intensity are more enjoyable for the athletes and provide a valuable carry-over into the game situation.

• Drills that introduce complex skills must be practiced initially at a slower tempo. When the skill is perfected the tempo is correspondingly increased until it reaches game intensity levels.

• Drills must be executed correctly. If the execution is not correct or a lack of effort is apparent the coach must stop the activity and emphasize the correct method and demand required training effort.

• Most drills allow competition which increases athletes' interest in practice and elevates the intensity of workout. Weaker players must be supported, which strengthens their self-esteem and increases their enthusiasm.

• Drills should flow from one to another with a minimum of time lost between drills. A well-planned drill progression flow makes an effective practice.

• Each drill should be evaluated after each practice. Were there noticeable improvements in the practiced skill levels of players?

Overview of technique and tactics

Charts 1 to 3 provide an overview of technical skills and offensive and defensive tactics for soccer. More detailed versions are discussed in the individual sections

Criteria to consider when working with individuals or groups

- **Speed:** Speed manifests itself in many ways beyond a player being able to move his body at a maximum rate. It is really a matter of the mind, how quickly a player is able to make decisions (i.e., in running and passing situations) and solve problems on the field.

- **Numbers:** Soccer is a game of numbers in the sense that a team needs to be able to make better decisions (in dribbling, passing, and goal scoring situations) and solve more problems in a given time (90 minutes) than the other team.

- **Perfection:** The factor that most decides the outcome of a game is which team makes the fewest mistakes (i.e., in dribbling and passing situations) in a given time.

- **Efficiency:** Who can complete the most tasks in a row without making a mistake? It is not enough for a team or a player to make excellent decisions in isolation from one another. There must be continuity in decision-making. Building one correct decision on another leads to scoring and preventing goals, and therefore, winning games.

Also keep in mind:

- Not every exercise should be competitive. The focus should be on mastery of individual techniques and team tactics at a controlled pace.

- Try to introduce technical and tactical drills in which players already possess most of the basic skills. It is difficult to make the most of drills that have a specific outcome in mind, when players are simultaneously learning more basic skills within those drills.

- Try to choose drills that are related to game situations.

Chart 1

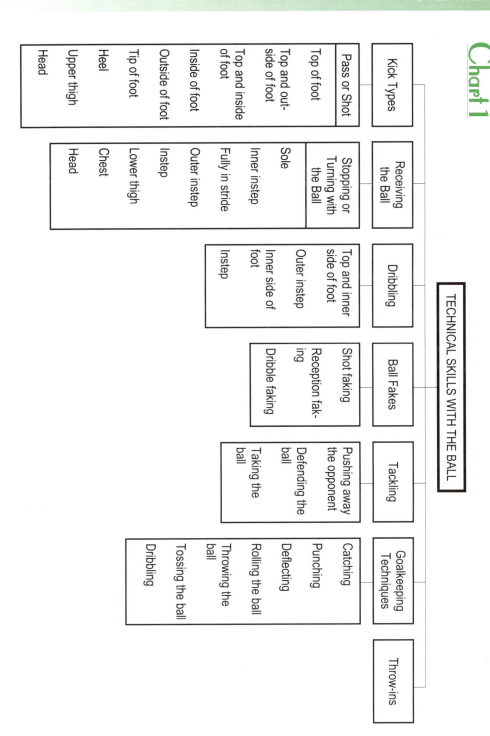

TECHNICAL SKILLS WITH THE BALL

Kick Types
- Pass or Shot
- Top of foot
- Top and out-side of foot
- Top and inside of foot
- Inside of foot
- Outside of foot
- Tip of foot
- Heel
- Upper thigh
- Head

Receiving the Ball
- Stopping or Turning with the Ball
- Sole
- Inner instep
- Fully in stride
- Outer instep
- Instep
- Lower thigh
- Chest
- Head

Dribbling
- Top and inner side of foot
- Outer instep
- Inner side of foot
- Instep

Ball Fakes
- Shot faking
- Reception fak-ing
- Dribble faking

Tackling
- Pushing away the opponent
- Defending the ball
- Taking the ball

Goalkeeping Techniques
- Catching
- Punching
- Deflecting
- Rolling the ball
- Throwing the ball
- Tossing the ball
- Dribbling

Throw-ins

Chart 2

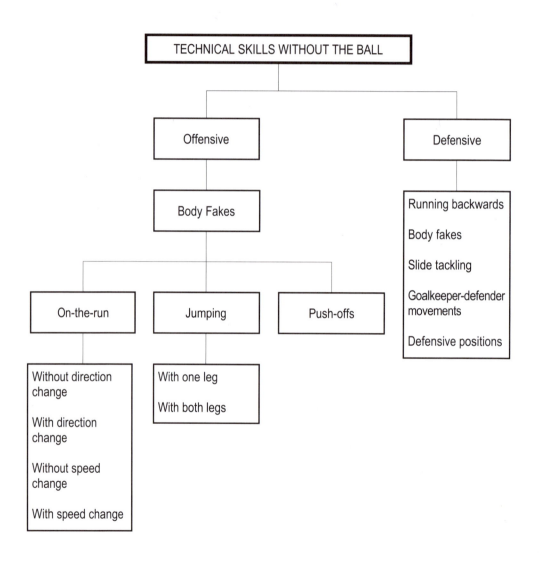

TECHNICAL SKILLS WITHOUT THE BALL

- Offensive
  - Body Fakes
    - On-the-run
      - Without direction change
      - With direction change
      - Without speed change
      - With speed change
    - Jumping
      - With one leg
      - With both legs
    - Push-offs
- Defensive
  - Running backwards
  - Body fakes
  - Slide tackling
  - Goalkeeper-defender movements
  - Defensive positions

Chart 3

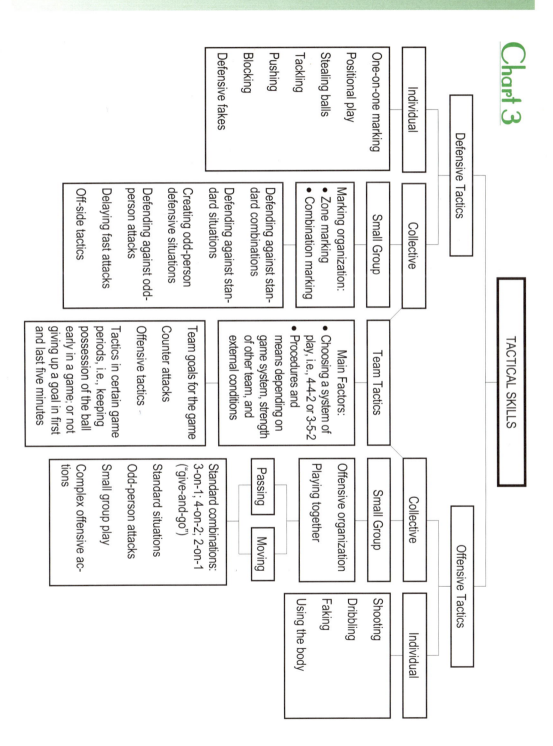

TACTICAL SKILLS

Defensive Tactics

Individual
- One-on-one marking
- Positional play
- Stealing balls
- Tackling
- Pushing
- Blocking
- Defensive fakes

Collective

Small Group
Marking organization:
- Zone marking
- Combination marking
- Defending against standard combinations
- Defending against standard situations
- Creating odd-person defensive situations
- Defending against odd-person attacks
- Delaying fast attacks
- Off-side tactics

Team Tactics
Main Factors:
- Choosing a system of play, i.e., 4-4-2 or 3-5-2
- Procedures and means depending on game system, strength of other team, and external conditions
- Team goals for the game
- Counter attacks
- Offensive tactics
- Tactics in certain game periods, i.e., keeping possession of the ball early in a game; or not giving up a goal in first and last five minutes

Offensive Tactics

Individual
- Shooting
- Dribbling
- Faking
- Using the body

Collective

Small Group
- Offensive organization
- Playing together

Passing
Moving

- Standard combinations: 3-on-1; 4-on-2; 2-on-1 ("give-and-go")
- Standard situations
- Odd-person attacks
- Small group play
- Complex offensive actions

Technique and individual tactics without the ball

Players must develop soccer-specific technical and tactical skills, including skills without the ball. These skills are summarized in **Chart 4**. For example, it is necessary to coordinate running without the ball with running with the ball. Technique of running without the ball should not be confused with general fitness training. Training designed to enhance soccer-specific running skills must be incorporated into practice and should include exercises that reflect the complex and varied tasks involved in soccer.

Running drills

1. Use positions on the field as starting points for running drills. Begin with a defender's position, such as "right back" (or any other soccer-specific position), and start the running out of this position.

2. Running with kicking movements of legs.

3. Running with speed changes (that simulate dribbling).

4. Running with fakes (e.g., make a step to the right and run to the left).

5. Running and slide tackling.

6. Running with jumps (simulating heading the ball).

7. Running forward with stops.

8. Running from a start either to the left or to the right (signal given at start).

9. Running backwards in a defensive position, beginning with a turn at the start.

10. One step forward and then running backwards.

Chart 4

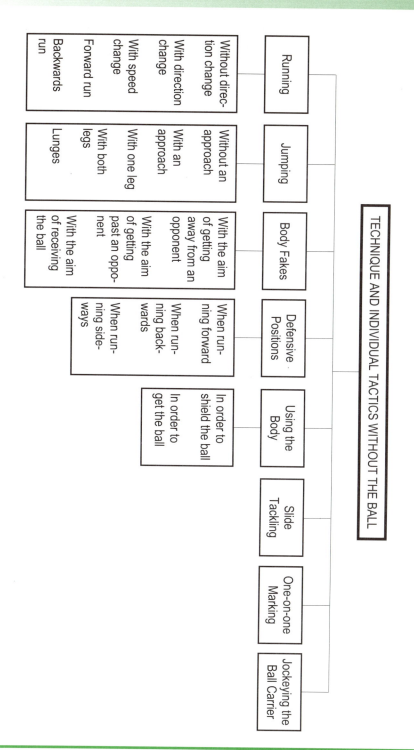

TECHNIQUE AND INDIVIDUAL TACTICS WITHOUT THE BALL

Running
- Without direction change
- With direction change
- With speed change
- Forward run
- Backwards run

Jumping
- Without an approach
- With an approach
- With one leg
- With both legs
- Lunges

Body Fakes
- With the aim of getting away from an opponent
- With the aim of getting past an opponent
- With the aim of receiving the ball

Defensive Positions
- When running forward
- When running backwards
- When running sideways

Using the Body
- In order to shield the ball
- In order to get the ball

Slide Tackling

One-on-one Marking

Jockeying the Ball Carrier

Jumping drills

11. Head-ball standing jumps.

12. Head-ball running jumps.

13. Head-ball jumps with a forward dive.

14. Jump with stretching one leg sideways after a short run sideways.

Bumping drills

15. Two players run next to each other and bump into each other with the shoulder.

16. Ten to fifteen players run around in a small field and bump into each other.

17. Player A has the ball. Player B runs next to player A and tries to get the ball away from player A. Player A bumps into player B and shields the ball.

18. Small field games with emphasis on pushing and bumping.

One-on-one defending and separating drills

19. Tag games inside a field. The chaser has to make sure he does not go out of bounds.

20. Partners face each other. Player A tries to pass player B with a fake; player B tries to stay in front of player A with quick moves.

21. Players A and B face each other a few metres apart, 40 to 60 metres from the goal. Player B tries to keep player A from running into the goal. Player A should be pushed to the outside.

22. Player A runs forward and player B runs backwards facing player A a few metres apart. Player A tries to pass player B. Player B tries to remain between the player and the goal.

23. Player A runs a few metres in front of player B. He or she changes speed or direction, stops, jumps, and starts whenever he or she wants. Player B has to imitate every movement.

24. One-on-one coverage in training games: players are only allowed to challenge the one player they have been assigned to mark.

Slide-tackling drills

25. Without a ball or opponent: practicing the technique of slide tackling.

26. With a resting ball.

27. Against a dribbling opponent.

28. As the opponent is receiving a ball.

29. Against an opponent shooting on goal.

Drills for challenging and pushing away opponents

30. Challenging dribbling opponents.

31. Challenging opponents as they receive a ball.

32. Challenging opponents during passes or shots on goal.

33. Challenging opponents by using body fakes.

34. Pushing dribbling opponents to the outside.

Technique and individual tactics with the ball

Getting used to the ball

Getting used to the ball requires learning "on-the-ball" techniques. The drills are mostly used in the beginning of a training session and are designed to develop a "feel for the ball" and ball control.

The following types of competitive drills can be used in practice:

• individual competition

• partner competition

• group competition: row with one ball passer, circle with one ball passer, circle without ball passer, square, rectangle, etc.

Instructional points

• Execute all drills thoroughly according to the coach's instructions (e.g., left foot, right foot, thigh-foot).

• Vary the types of drills used to develop the same general skills.

• Emphasize correct body technique as an important basis for successful ball control.

Exercises

1. Roll the ball forward with the sole of the shoe. The player's body weight rests on the other, jumping leg.

2. The ball is dribbled with the sole. The player moves in a forward direction, using the sole of the shoes to move the ball between right foot and left.

3. Balancing the ball with the foot or head. The ball is either put on the head or foot. It can be caught balancing after throwing it up, passing it back and forth from one foot to the other, or from partner to partner.

4. Balancing the ball with the feet:
- Randomly
- With one foot
- With the left and right foot, alternately
- Twice with each foot, alternately
- With one foot, while jumping up and down on the other foot
- In a group or with a partner

5. Balancing the ball with the upper thigh:
- Randomly
- On one thigh
- Alternately left and right

6. Balancing the ball on the head:
- Individually
- With a partner or in a group

7. Balancing with the foot, thigh, and head:
- Randomly with the head and thigh
- With the feet and thighs alternately
- With the foot and thigh of one leg
- With the feet, thigh, and head in a certain order, or randomly

8. Other aids can be used, such as a ball pendulum or a target wall. See SoccerPal section beginning on page 151.

Passing and shooting

Passing

Passing is one of the most important components of effective team play. When mastered, passing is the one skill that can most directly affect the quality and outcome of a game. Passing is also vital to setting up another crucial skill in soccer, shooting. Therefore, it is important for players to master the most common kick types. **Chart 5** presents a breakdown of passing and shooting skills.

The majority of drills should be practiced with a partner and should include all of the possible variations of kick types, pace, direction, etc. The drills should also be connected to other drills or skill areas as soon as possible (e.g., receiving the ball and passing; possession of the ball and passing, passing and position changes, etc.).

Instructional points

• Keep the different functions of the standing leg and kicking leg in mind.

• Practice technique with both the right and left foot.

• A player's first instinct should be to pass the ball with the instep.

• Do not use more force than is necessary.

• Precision of passing is more important than speed.

• During the movement of play, players should constantly be aware of the various positions of teammates, in order to be able to select the best possible passing option.

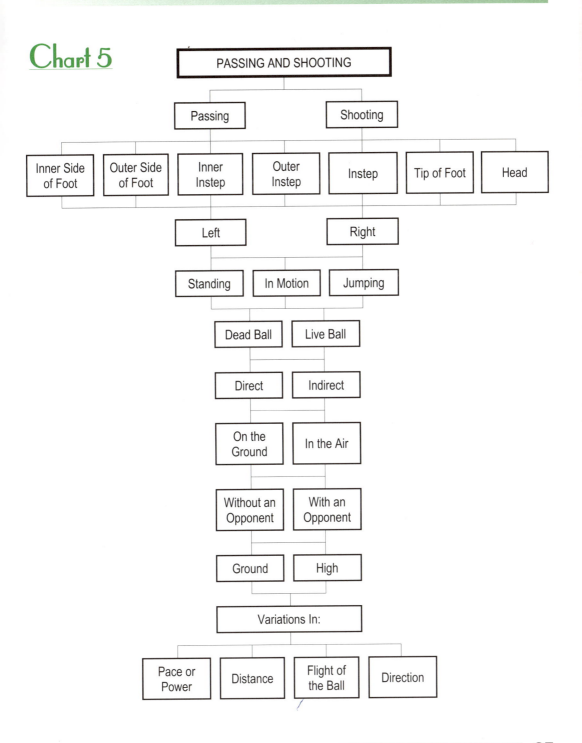

Chart 5

PASSING AND SHOOTING

Passing — Shooting

Inner Side of Foot — Outer Side of Foot — Inner Instep — Outer Instep — Instep — Tip of Foot — Head

Left — Right

Standing — In Motion — Jumping

Dead Ball — Live Ball

Direct — Indirect

On the Ground — In the Air

Without an Opponent — With an Opponent

Ground — High

Variations In:

Pace or Power — Distance — Flight of the Ball — Direction

Shooting

Shooting is the most critical of the individual offensive skills. In modern soccer, every player, regardless of position, needs to be able to shoot well. Just as with passing, shooting involves a variety of kick types and styles.

There are two main types of shooting practice:

- Shooting at targets (which places an emphasis on precision and technical execution of different types of shots).

- Shooting at a goal with a goalkeeper (which involves more of a sense of game situations—tactics—and how players react to those situations to either score goals or prevent them).

Instructional points

- A player should focus on the proper positioning and movement of both the still foot and the kicking foot.

- Successful shooting requires the precise control of the player's kicking motion and the accurate delivery of the ball to its target.

- A player should keep his or her eyes on the ball when shooting.

- If possible, a player should take into account the position and the behaviour of the goalkeeper before shooting.

- A player should practice shooting in complex drills and game-related situations.

- A player's kicking leg should follow-through towards the intended target after contact with the ball.

D1 **Dead-ball shooting** The coach should organize each of the following six shooting situations separately:

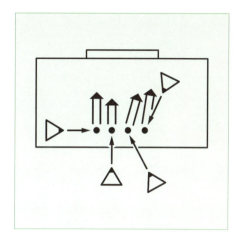

• a direct run and shot
• an angled run and shot
• a run from the side and shot
• a run from the goal-side, with a turn and a shot
• rapid-fire shooting
• random shooting from wherever the balls sit

The first four positions are shown in the diagram.
Players should be made aware of the unique nature of each position, type of shot, and style of
shooting. Note that in this drill the balls are not
moving or being passed; instead, balls are being placed in position, then approached by
the players. Players should ideally be lined up in rows in one position, then be signaled
to move towards the ball, strike it, retrieve it, and go to the back of their rows to complete their assigned number of repetitions.

D2 **Shooting off a pass** Players shoot in the
following situations:

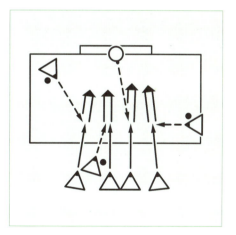

• a direct shot
• a shot with an angle
• a shot from the side
• on an approach from goal-side of the ball—a
  shot with an angle
• a shot from goal-side of the ball—with a sharp
  turn

The coach will again organize each situation
separately. Players will be expected to take all
shots first-time, with no additional touch for control. The coach can provide the passing service or
assign a player, who will rotate out of the passing position at a regular interval.

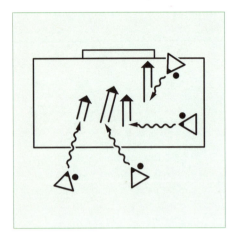

D3 <u>Shooting with or without a change of direction</u> Players line up in a row and begin their dribble from the four positions shown in the diagram:

- towards the goal
- at an angle to the goal
- parallel to the goal
- away from the goal

Each position will be dealt with separately. Once each player has attempted five to ten shots from a position, a row will be set up at a new position with new instructions from the coach.

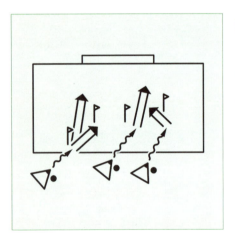

D4<u>Shooting with static obstacles</u> Players line up in rows and are asked to dribble at a fast pace towards an obstacle (such as a flag or cone), change direction, then shoot. Five to ten shots per obstacle position are recommended. Training with static obstacles will prepare players for having to deal with active opposition in later drills and game situations.

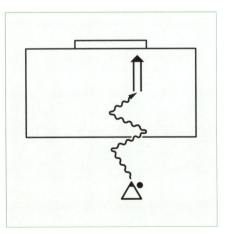

D5 <u>Shooting with a change of direction, but no opposition</u> Lined up in a row approximately 35 metres from goal, players must dribble, execute a change of direction at the 18-yard box, such as an exaggerated zig-zag, then shoot on goal.

D6 **Shooting against active opponents who:**
- approach from behind
- approach from the side
- approach at an angle
- approach from the front

Each position should be organized separately by the coach, with attackers and defenders doing at least five repetitions per position. Since the opponents are active, the coach will want to provide instructional points to defenders as well as the attackers, who are working on their shooting.

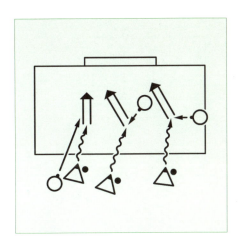

D7 **Shooting (one- or two-touch) after receiving a low direct pass**
The low pass can come from the goal line from a defender at one of the posts, who can also provide passive opposition. Shooters stand in a row ten metres above the 18-yard box, and approach the pass for a shot from the top of the box. They should not be given any particular instructions regarding the style of kick; however, the coach should emphasize first-time contact and a shot that at least hits the net.

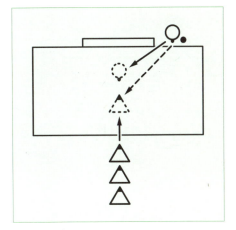

D8 **Shooting after receiving a low pass from the side**
Half of the players stand to one side of the 18-yard box as passers, while the other half stand at the top of the box as shooters. After each pass and shot, players switch lines. One touch is permitted to control the pass from the side, emphasizing close control. The touch is allowed because of the angle and uncertainty of the quality of the pass; however, players are encouraged to take the first-time shot because this shot is always preferred in the box—both defenders and goalkeepers have more difficulty with a quick shot taken on the first touch.

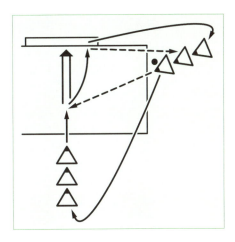

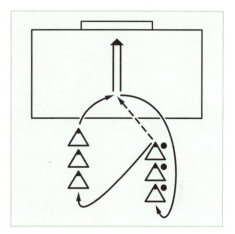

D9 Shooting after receiving a low pass from behind   Facing the goal, with the pass coming from behind, players could let the ball roll on for a first-time shot. However, given the degree of difficulty for such a shot, taking one touch before shooting is recommended. The coach should set up this drill so that the passing row is at least ten yards behind the receiving row. Receivers will have to step away from the line in order to receive the pass from behind and have a clear shot on goal. Passers and shooters switch lines after each shot.

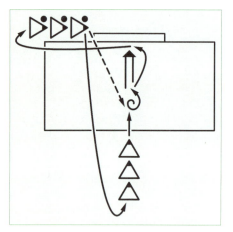

D10 Shooting after receiving a low pass on-the-turn   With players divided into two rows (one for passing, one for shooting), the shooter should show for the ball at the top of the 18-yard box. The shooter will take one touch and simultaneously complete a full turn with the ball, facing the goal from a new angle. The next touch is a shot on goal. Only two touches are permitted. Shooter and passer switch lines after each shot.

D11 Shooting after receiving a high pass with the thigh   Players are divided into a passing and shooting row, set up around the top of the 18-yard box, with players switching lines after each pass and shot. Service will be by hand to ensure consistency. With his or her back to the goal, the player will take one touch for control with the thigh, then either do a full-volley (not permitting the ball to hit the ground) or a half-volley (striking the ball as it hits the ground) shot at goal.

Given a low player-coach ratio, the scenario could also involve having the coach provide frequent service of numerous balls to individual players. For example, given ten balls and two players, a coach could feed those ten balls quickly to one player and have the other player retrieve balls. The two players would switch after every ten shots at goal.

D12 <u>Shooting after receiving a high pass with the chest</u> Similar to the previous drill (D11), except service is to the chest. After the first touch, players either do a full-volley (not permitting the ball to hit the ground) or a half-volley (striking the ball as it hits the ground) shot at goal.

Given a low player-coach ratio, the scenario could also involve having the coach provide frequent service of numerous balls to individual players. For example, given ten balls and two players, a coach could feed those ten balls quickly to one player and have the other player retrieve balls. The two players would switch after every ten shots at goal.

D13 <u>Shooting after receiving a high pass with the head</u> Similar to above, except players control the ball with heir heads, before taking a shot at goal (not headed directly at goal). Ideally, the ball should fall within a close zone of control so the player can either quickly spin and shoot, or run on to the ball for a shot.

D14 <u>Shooting after a roll forwards or backwards</u> This drill introduces players to the often ignored, but ever-present, acrobatic nature of the game. Players line up in one row above the 18-yard box. They perform a gymnastic forward roll as part of their run up to a dead ball placed at the top of the box by the coach.

D15 <u>Shooting after jumping over one or more hurdles</u> One way to set up this drill is to use players as hurdles. Each player could be assigned a number. When the coach calls out a number, the player with that number jumps up, runs to the back of the line of kneeling players, jumps over the players, then shoots the dead ball placed at the top of the 18-yard box, on goal.

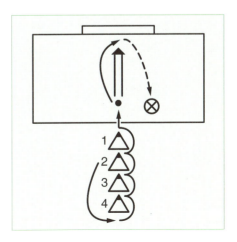

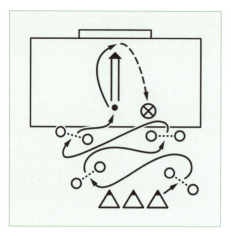

D16 **<u>Shooting after a slalom around several obstacles</u>** Players negotiate a series of gates marked by cones, then shoot a dead-ball on goal from the top of the 18-yard box. This drill could be timed and evaluated to give players incentive to perform all aspects well, i.e., running for pace, negotiating obstacles without error, and shooting to score.

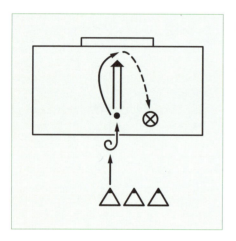

D17 **<u>Shooting after a run-and-turn</u>** The first player takes off at maximum pace from a row of players approximately 30 metres away from goal. The player executes a full 360° turn at the top of the 18-yard box, then strikes a dead ball just inside the box, at goal.

D18 **<u>Shooting after getting up from a seated position</u>** All players are seated in a row at the top of the 18-yard box. After the coach has placed a ball in front of the first player in line, he or she springs up, shoots at the goal, then joins the back of the line. This drill could also serve as a rapid-fire drill for goalkeepers. To keep the drill running efficiently, players should collect all balls shot wide of the goal.

D19 **Shooting after vaulting over another player**   One player stands in a crouched position with his or her knees supporting the hands, two metres in front of a row of players standing approximately 25 metres from the goal. Players straddle over his or her back and shoot a dead ball on goal. After the row of players has gone through once, the player serving as the vault is changed.

D20 **Shooting after five push-ups**   Starting from a row of players just above the 18-yard box, players perform five proper and quick push-ups, then launch themselves into shooting a dead ball (placed by the coach) on goal. Players either collect balls going wide of the goal or go directly to the back of the line.

Receiving the ball

To effectively receive a ball, players must be able to control the ball in a position to make the next move (a dribble, pass, or shot) without losing possession. Correct reception is dependent upon the player's first-touch or ball-control skills (such as being able to cushion a ball with the laces of the shoe, the thigh, the chest, or the head) (see **Chart 6**).

Basic drills should initially be practiced with a partner. All of the different variations should be attempted. Also, when practicing with a partner, ball reception should take on increasing complexity, such as:

• receiving the ball, then passing back to the partner
• receiving the ball, then making a long, lead pass to a moving player
• receiving the ball, then taking a shot on goal.

When it is not possible to train with a partner, players can use a variety of independent drills:

• the ball is "thrown in" against a wall and controlled (by the foot, thigh, chest, or head)
• the ball is thrown up into the air, controlled, then dribbled away
• the ball is thrown up and controlled by a player who gets up from a seated position
• the ball is thrown up and controlled by a player who simulates faking an opponent.

Instructional points

• A player should move towards the ball when receiving a pass, rather than waiting for the ball to arrive.

• A player should always attempt to get to the ball as fast as possible.

• A player should always be in motion and aim to receive the ball while in motion.

• Upon receiving the ball, players should make it a habit of immediately moving with the ball in a direction that advances the team.

• To maintain the best possible ball control, players should always try to keep the ball on the ground.

Chart 6

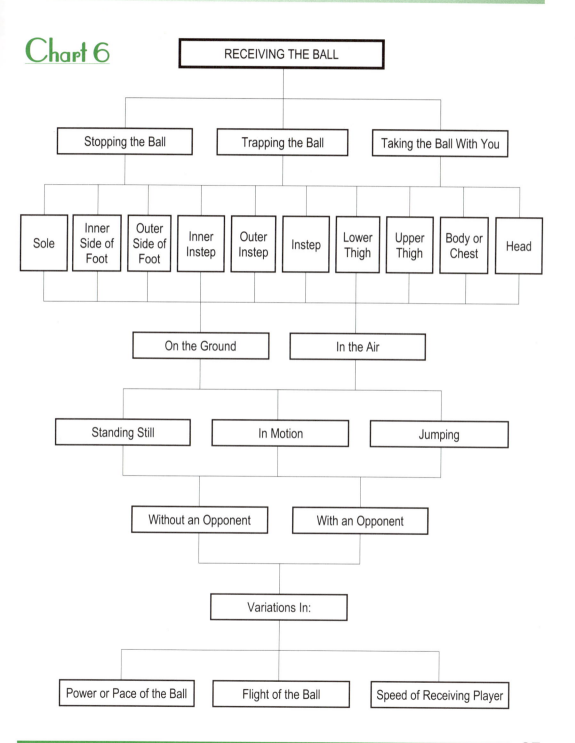

RECEIVING THE BALL

- Stopping the Ball
- Trapping the Ball
- Taking the Ball With You

| Sole | Inner Side of Foot | Outer Side of Foot | Inner Instep | Outer Instep | Instep | Lower Thigh | Upper Thigh | Body or Chest | Head |

- On the Ground
- In the Air

- Standing Still
- In Motion
- Jumping

- Without an Opponent
- With an Opponent

Variations In:

- Power or Pace of the Ball
- Flight of the Ball
- Speed of Receiving Player

Dribbling

Dribbling consists of players maintaining control of the ball with various parts of the feet while in motion (see **Chart 7**). Effective dribbling requires that players not only maintain control and move with the ball, but that they also comfortably maintain a clear view of the direction in which they are moving. This means that for at least a portion of the dribbling time, players should be able to keep their heads up while dribbling.

When performed with a high degree of skill, and particularly when going forward on the attack, dribbling can give individuals and teams an important edge in a game.

Instructional points

• Players should always keep the ball close to their feet when being covered by an opponent.

• Players should not simply dribble and look to see where they are going; they should also pay attention to how the play is developing and be able to correctly decide what the next optimal move would be.

• Players should always carry the ball with the foot that is furthest away from the opponent.

• Players should not dribble if they do not have a purpose.

• Fakes and changes in speed are important factors for dribbling.

D21 **Dribbling straight ahead:**
• with one foot
• with both feet alternately
• with a high frequency of ball contact
• without looking at the ball too much.

Chart 7

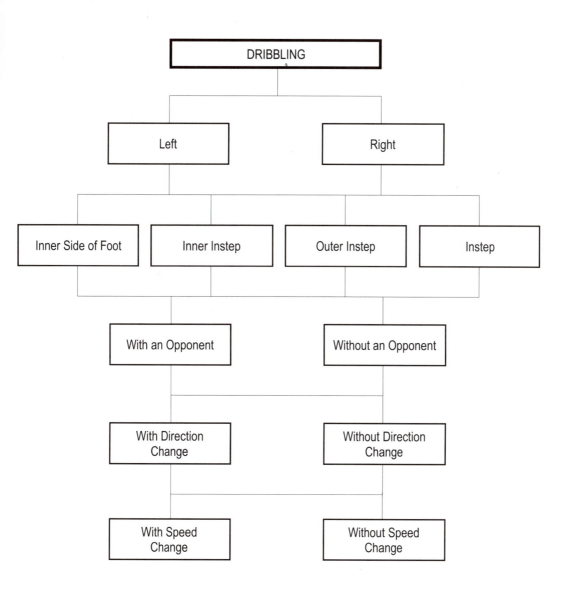

D22 **Dribbling with constant direction change**   The ball is dribbled with constant direction change. The coach should instruct players to make sharp, diagonal and lateral movements every five to ten metres.

D23 **Dribbling with irregular direction change**   Players dribble around a designated area using irregular and random direction changes. To enhance the drill, the coach can place cones in random fashion around the training area. Players would then move around the area and dribble towards and around the cones at their choosing. The coach should ensure that the pace is fast and the direction changes are sharp.

D24 **Dribbling with sudden, irregular direction change**   Players dribble around a designated area using sudden, irregular direction changes. Such direction changes could be 180° turns that occur at the signal of the coach. The drill could progress to another stage whereby the direction change could be combined with a change of pace and short run that occurs after the change of direction.

D25 **Dribbling vs. a passive defender**   The ball is dribbled against a passive opponent, with the dribbler attempting to quickly use both feet to unsettle the defender. The progression in this drill is then to have the ball kept under control and dribbled against an active opponent. Players switch roles frequently.

D26 **Change of pace 1v1**   In pairs, one player starts with the ball and uses a change of pace to get past a defender and tries to play the ball through a marked area or to score a goal.

D27 **Dribbling in confined space**   Eight to twelve players dribble in a small confined space performing changes of direction and pace on the coach's whistle. The players must make sharp movements and avoid any contact with other players as they move around in the area .

D28 Dribble past the line   An offensive player tries to dribble past a single defender across a designated goal line. Players switch roles after each attempt.

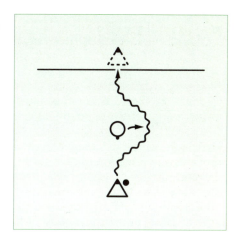

Faking—Developing 1v1 moves

Fakes are an important part of every player's repertoire. All position-players (attackers, midfielders, defenders, and goalkeepers) need to be able to employ fakes in order to gain an advantage over opponents in a variety of game situations.

Ball fakes consist of a player giving an opponent the impression that he or she is going to move in one direction or do one thing, when in fact he or she intends to move in another direction or do something else. Fakes are therefore a practice in deception. The goal of the player who fakes is to unsettle his opponent, create a weakness in the defence, and take advantage of a new opportunity. Learning to fake well requires experience and knowledge of how and when to utilize fakes effectively. **Chart 8** presents a summary of the various faking skills.

It is important to make fakes as realistic as possible. You want the defender to believe you are going to do what you are faking to do. A fake should approximate the actual movement (speed, positioning, and direction) as closely as possible. To be effective, the transition from fake to intended action must be smooth and quick; otherwise, a defender can usually distinguish between a deceptive movement (fake) and an intended action.

Instructional points

- Players must make the fake look real. Every fake must be executed with intensity and a quick, sudden movement.

- Players should only learn and practice fakes that can be used in a game.

- It is better for players to use a smaller number of well-developed fakes than to attempt a wider variety of less effective ones.

- Players should learn to choose the fake that is appropriate for the game situation.

Chart 8

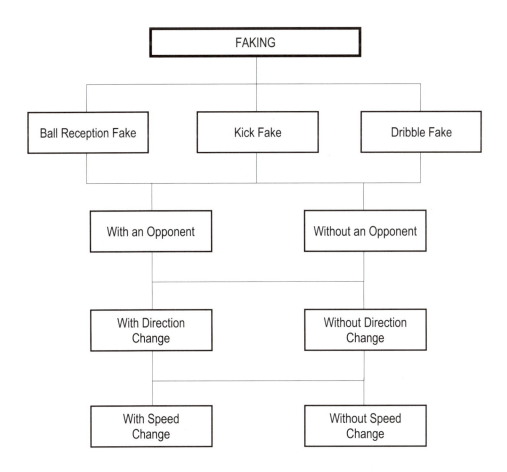

Ball reception fakes

The most effective way to practice ball reception fakes or moves is to have a drill where players move sharply towards the passed ball.

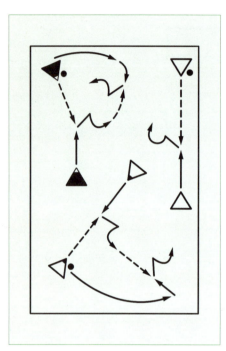

D29 Ball reception fake In partners, players move around a designated area, sharing one ball. The player without the ball approaches the ball carrier from approximately 20 metres, calling for the ball. While the ball is in flight, the receiver moves sharply towards the ball with a specific body posture, then changes that posture simultaneously with the first touch of the ball. The first touch of the ball coincides with a change of direction and pace. The drill is repeated continuously with the passer becoming the receiver. There should be constant motion from the partners and constant observation and feedback from the coach or trainer.

Pre-reception fakes

It is also useful for players to use fakes before they have an opportunity to receive the ball. In fact, fakes can be used to **create** ball reception opportunities. Faking can be used to shake-off, elude, or trick a close marker or defender. Effective faking can therefore create space and time for ball reception.

D30 **Fake to get open**   Players are divided into pairs with one ball between each pair. The player without the ball makes his or her move or fake **before** the ball is passed. The ball receiver moves towards the passer, stops suddenly, fakes in one direction, moves back in the direction of the passer, who then passes the ball. Upon receiving the ball, the player can then also perform the fake described in the previous drill (D29), changing direction and moving into a dribble.

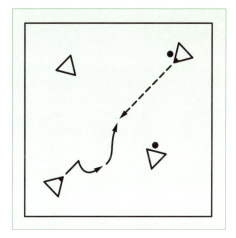

Shooting fakes

A shooting fake can have the effect of unsettling the opponent, whose first priority is to prevent a goal. By forcing the opponent to focus on this priority, he or she is then distracted from other dangers, such as an opportunistic pass to a teammate who is in a better position to shoot directly at goal.

D31 **Shot fake**   When running towards a passed ball, a player will fake a pass or shot on goal, then control the ball for an instant, before finally passing or dribbling the ball. When dribbling the ball forward, a pass or a shot is faked, and instead, the ball is stepped-on, dragged back, and finally dribbled with a sharp change of direction.

Dribbling fakes

Dribbling fakes have the effect of keeping the opponent at bay. Changes in direction and fakes ensure that the opponent is less able to threaten the ball carrier's objective—to maintain possession of the ball and move into more opportunistic areas of the opponent's half of the field.

D32 **Dribble fake**   A certain direction is faked by the ball carrier, and then the ball is dribbled in a different direction. When the opponent runs next to the player, the player can fake leaving the ball behind by stepping over it with the right foot. The ball is, however, taken up by the left foot without decreasing speed.

Throw-ins

The throw-in has become an integral part of offensive strategy in modern soccer. There-fore, throw-in drills should be integrated within a team's philosophy on "possession" and all "re-starts," such as free-kicks and corner-kicks. It is useful to integrate throw-ins into small-sided practice lead-up games and drills.

While in some team systems a throw-in specialist is used due to the tactical advantage a strong throw can provide, the following are throw-in drills with an emphasis on receiving the ball. These drills are designed to develop a better technical sense in players of how to get to, and then distribute, a throw-in pass.

Instructional points

- It is preferred that throw-in passes be directed to a receiver's feet.

- However, in game situations, the ball can be passed to a receiver's chest and head if the situation calls for it.

- Ensure that players focus on precision and not power in throwing in the ball.

- Ensure that players are conscious of throw-in rules when executing extremely short throw-ins: the ball must travel from all the way behind the head to all the way in front of the head.

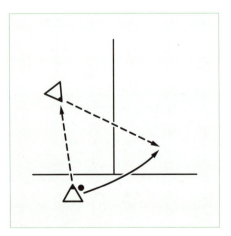

D33 Back to the thrower The ball is thrown in to a player, who passes it right back to the player who threw in the ball.

D34 <u>Receive and dribble</u> The ball is thrown in to a player, who controls the ball, then moves into a dribble.

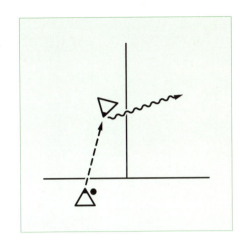

D35 <u>Fake and dribble or pass back</u> The ball is thrown in to a player, who fakes a move and dribbles away, or passes the ball back to the player who threw the ball into play.

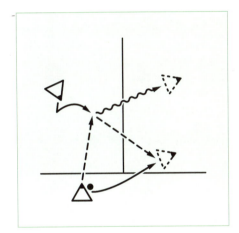

D36 <u>Move towards the thrower</u> The ball is thrown in to a player, who makes a sharp, close movement towards the thrower.

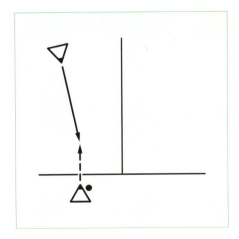

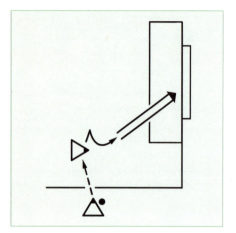

D37 Fake and shoot The ball is thrown in to a player, who fakes a move, then takes a shot on goal.

Combined skill drills

Soccer training should aspire to the same level of technical and tactical complexity as is found in game situations. While many of the drills in this book are aimed at individual technical development, the greater goal is to have players combining a variety of technical skills in game-like situations.

Instructional points

- Precision and technically accurate performance are preferred over speed.

- During combined skill drills, players should not be given any specific technical instructions (e.g., "Use the laces of your shoe to pass the ball."). At this stage, technical skills should come naturally to players. In these complex, game-like drills, players should focus more on issues such as positioning and decision-making (when to sprint; when to stop; when to pass; when to shoot; etc.).

- Choose exercises that are appropriate for the players' skill level.

- Application of the drills should vary according to coaching style and skill level of players. However, when training players, have in mind their short and long-term technical development.

Passing and receiving

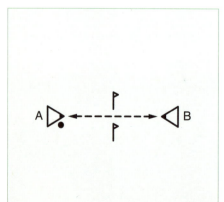

D38 **Through the passage** Player A and player B pass the ball back and forth through a narrow passage marked by flags or cones. *Variation:* player A and player B pass the ball back and forth at a distance of 20 to 25 metres, between two cones, past a player in the middle who tries to head the ball.

D39 **Pass, run, receive** Player A and player B pass the ball back and forth through flags (or cones) while running along a marked path. Players should practice passing through the flags in both directions and using both feet. *Variation*: the ball is played twice through the same passage.

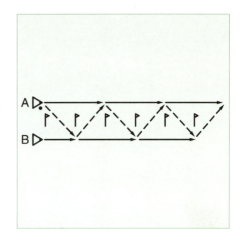

D40 **Two-person pass and move** Players are divided into pairs. Player A begins with the ball and passes to player B, who alternates sides after each pass. Player B delivers a return pass to player A before switching sides to receive the next pass. Players switch roles after ten passes have been completed.

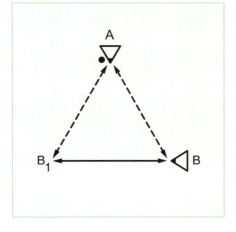

D41 **Move and pass around the middle** Players are divided into pairs and given one ball between them. Player B moves around player A in a circular pattern, passing the ball back and forth with player A in the middle. Players switch roles after completing two full circles or twelve passes.

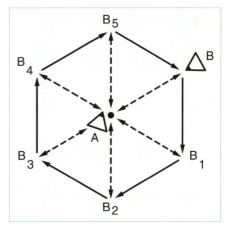

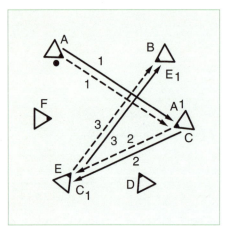

D42 Pass and follow around the circle Approximately six players stand in a circle. Player A randomly passes the ball to another player in the circle and follows the pass. Every player who passes the ball follows their pass and takes the new position in the circle. The drill continues until every player has received at least five passes.

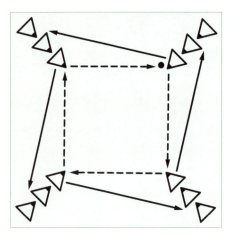

D43 Rows around the square Players stand in a square formation, three players in each corner. The ball is passed around the square in one direction. After passing the ball, players run to join the end of the group in the opposite direction of the pass (e.g., pass right, go left).

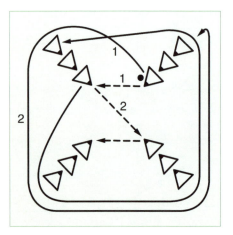

D44 Pass and run around the square Players stand in a square formation, three players in each corner. The ball is randomly passed to another player in the square. After each pass, players sprint around the square and rejoin the end of the same line.

D45 Pass and diagonal run Players stand in a square formation, two or more players in each corner. The ball is passed around the square in one direction. After each pass, players run diagonally to join the end of the line in the opposite corner.

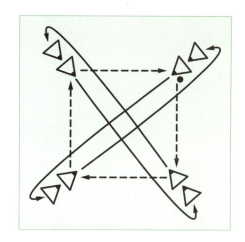

D46 Pass and slow follow Two rows of three players are formed and stand facing each other approximately 25 metres apart. Player A passes the ball to player B, and follows the ball slowly to join the end of the opposite row. Player B passes the ball over the approaching player A, to the front of the opposite row, and runs slowly to the other side, and so on, until every player has passed the ball at least four times.

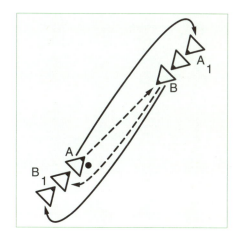

D47 Octagonal pass and cross Eight players form an octagon. One pair of players facing each other in the octagon are each given a ball. At the given signal, the balls are passed at the same time, in the same direction around the octagon. After passing the ball, players switch positions with the player directly opposite them.

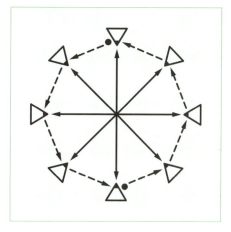

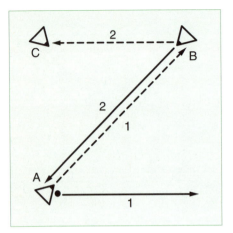

D48 <u>Lateral and diagonal</u> Three players occupy three corners of a square. Player A passes the ball diagonally to player B, and runs to the unoccupied corner of the square. Player B passes the ball to player C, and runs diagonally to fill the position vacated by player A. Players who receive a diagonal pass, pass it on laterally. Players who receive a lateral pass, pass it on diagonally. After each pass, players always run to the unoccupied corner of the square.

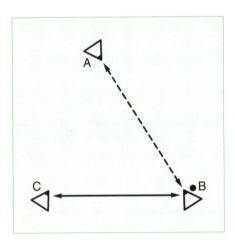

D49 <u>Lateral switch and feed</u> Three players each occupy one corner of a triangle. Player A at the top of the triangle passes the ball to player B in one corner, who passes back to player A, and quickly switches positions with player C in the other corner. Player A then passes the ball to player C (now in the position previously held by player B), who passes the ball back to player A, and switches again with player B. Player A continues in the role of feeder at the top of the triangle for a set number of repetitions, then switches roles with either player B or player C.

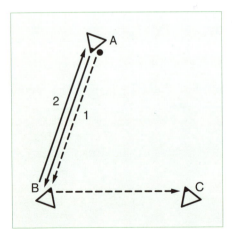

D50 <u>Follow and fill</u> Three players each occupy one corner of a triangle. Player A passes to player B and follows the pass to occupy position B. Player B passes the ball to player C, and runs to the position recently vacated by player A. Player C then passes the ball to player A and follows the pass, and so on. The drill consists of alternating between following the ball and running to occupy an empty position. When performed correctly, each player alternately follows his or her pass, and runs to occupy the empty position in the triangle.

D51 **Fill the gap**   Three players occupy three corners of a square as shown. Player A passes the ball to the empty corner to the right, where the ball is accepted by player B (who has run down to accept it). After passing the ball, player A runs diagonally across the square to fill the position vacated by player B. Player B then passes the ball to the now empty corner to the left, where the ball is accepted by player C (who has run down to accept it). After passing the ball, player B runs diagonally to fill the position vacated by player C, and so on. Players follow this pattern until 20 successful passes have been completed.

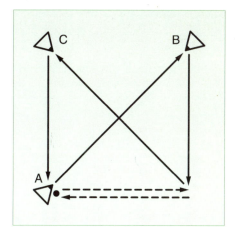

Passing, receiving, and dribbling

D52 **Dribble, pass, and switch**   Players stand in two facing rows. Player A dribbles the ball ahead several metres, then passes to player B (another several metres away), and runs to join the end of the opposite row. After receiving the ball, player B dribbles ahead several metres in the other direction, passes to player C in the facing row, and runs to join the end of the opposite row, and so on. *Variations*: (a) after dribbling and passing, players run to the end of the same row; (b) a defender stands between the two rows trying to disrupt the dribble and pass.

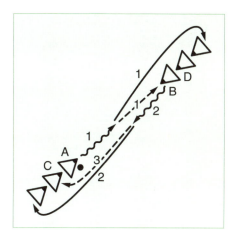

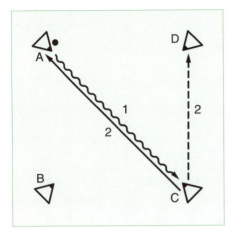

D53 Diagonal dribble and pass off Four players each occupy one corner of a square. Player A dribbles diagonally towards player C, passes the ball off, and takes the position of player C. Player C then passes the ball to player D to the right, and runs to fill the vacated position previously held by player A. Player D dribbles the ball diagonally towards player B, passes the ball off, and takes the position of player B. Player B then passes the ball to the left, runs to the empty position, and so on.

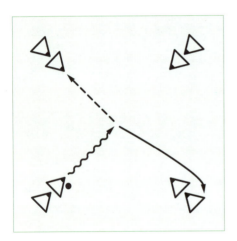

D54 Dribble, pass left, go right There are two players in every corner of a square. The ball is dribbled to the middle of the square and passed to the first player in the group to the left. After passing the ball, players join the end of the group to the right.

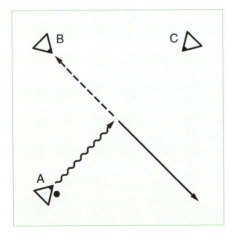

D55 Dribble, pass, and fill right Three players each occupy one corner of a square. Player A dribbles the ball to the middle of the square, passes it to player B to the left, and runs to the right to the unoccupied corner of the square. Player B accepts the ball, dribbles to the middle, passes to player C to the left, and runs to the right to the unoccupied part of the square, and so on.

D56 <u>Dribble, pass left, switch sides</u> Two players occupy every corner of a square. The first player in one group dribbles the ball to the middle of the square, passes to the first player to the left, and runs to the end of the group directly opposite him or her.

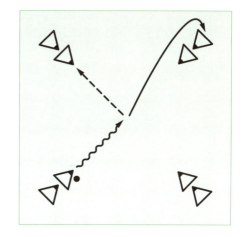

D57 <u>Dribble, pass left, move to empty corner</u> Three players each occupy one corner of a square. Player B dribbles the ball to the middle of the square, passes to player C to the left, and runs straight ahead to the unoccupied corner of the square.

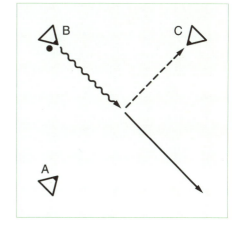

D58 <u>Dribble and diagonal pass</u> Three players occupy three corners of a square. Player A dribbles to the right to the unoccupied corner, and passes the ball diagonally to player B in the opposite corner. Player B then dribbles the ball to the right, and so on.

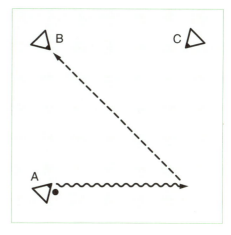

Shooting within combined drills

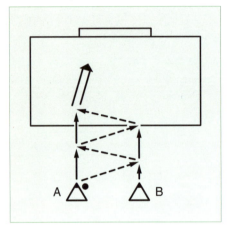

D59 Diagonal pass and shoot Two players move towards the goal with diagonal passes. Just after entering the 18-yard box, one player shoots on goal.

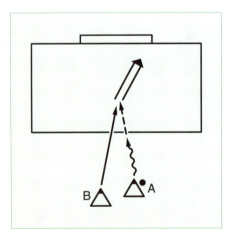

D60 Laying off to the trailing player Player A dribbles the ball towards the goal with player B running behind or next to him or her. When player A lays a short pass forward, player B immediately sprints forward and takes a first-time shot on goal.

D61 __18-yard box give-and-go__   Player A dribbles the ball ahead slowly and passes to player B, standing just inside the 18-yard box. Player B returns a pass back to player A, who moves forward to receive the ball in motion. The give-and-go is completed with a shot on goal by player A.

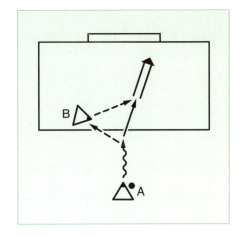

D62 __Give-and-go fake and shot__   Player A dribbles the ball ahead slowly and passes to player B, standing just inside the 18-yard box. Player B receives the pass from player A, fakes a give-and-go, and shoots at the goal on a quick turn.

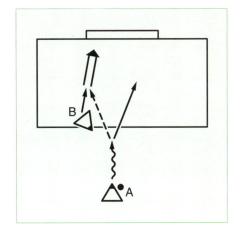

D63 __Laying up the ball for a shot__   Player A dribbles forward, lays the ball past a (passive or active) defender B, and shoots on goal.

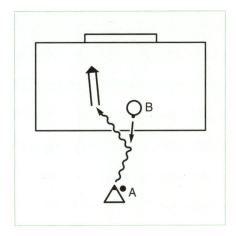

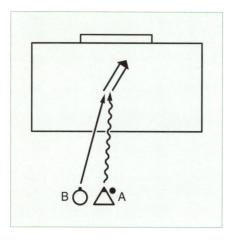

D64 <u>Defender pursuit</u> Starting from the same distance from goal, player A tries to shoot on goal while being pursued and disrupted by player B. Player A cannot attempt a shot until entering the 18-yard box.

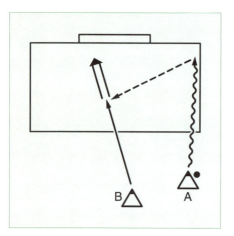

D65 <u>Cut back and shot</u> Player A dribbles the ball along the edge of the 18-yard box until almost reaching the goal line, then cuts the ball back towards player B at the penalty spot, who takes a first-time shot on goal.

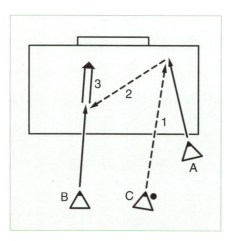

D66 <u>Deep pass and cut back</u> Player A receives a pass from player C close to the goal line, and cuts the ball back towards player B, who arrives at the penalty spot to take a first-time shot on goal.

D67 **Passive convergence** Attacker A and defender B start at the same time towards a ball
played forward into the top of the 18-yard box by
player C. Player A shoots on goal, with passive
opposition from player B.

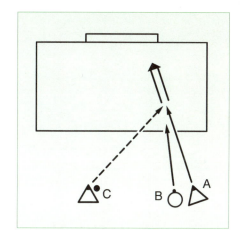

D68 **One-touch turn-and-shoot** Player A is
goal-side of the ball and runs out from the goal
towards a ball played by player B to the top of the
18-yard box. Player A takes one touch with a
quick simultaneous turn and shoots on goal.

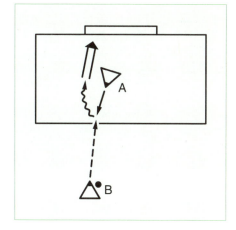

D69 **Give-and-go for a first-time shot**
Player A runs out from the goal towards a ball
dribbled by player B. Player A receives a short
pass from player B and completes a give-and-go
with player B, who takes a first-time shot on goal.

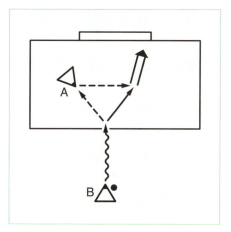

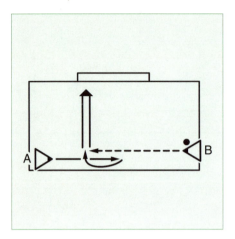

D70 Top of the box square ball Player B plays a square ball along the top of the box to player A, who runs to meet it half-way, then "dummies" the ball, letting it pass between his or her legs. As soon as the ball is past him or her, player A turns quickly and executes a first-time shot on goal.

1v1 drills to practice technique and individual tactics

The following drills should be practiced until all basic skills are part of the player's repertoire. Initially, cones or passive players are used as opponents. Next, defenders perform a kind of shadow defending, to force attackers to seek solutions without actually having to worry about losing the ball. And finally, the opponents are as active as they would be in games, and the attackers are challenged to find solutions, or risk losing possession of the ball.

Instructional points

- 1v1 drills represent the most effective learning environment for developing a diverse repertoire of fakes.

- Specific fakes should be used in specific situations.

- Initially, physical and speed aspects in drills should be de-emphasized.

- Where there will be shooting, the coach should place an emphasis on balls hitting the goal.

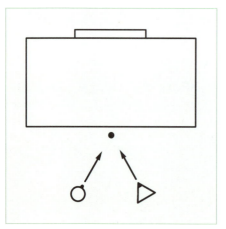

D71 **First to ball, first to shoot** Two players, a few metres away from each other, run towards a ball that is the same distance away from both players, at the top of the box. The first player to get to the ball is to attempt a shot on goal.

D72 **Shooting with a trailing player**   From a distance of about 30 metres, a player dribbles the ball towards the goal and, from about 11 metres out, attempts a shot on goal. A second player begins a few metres behind him and tries to disrupt the shot.

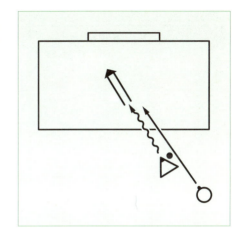

D73 **Headers**   A ball is thrown high to two players standing next to each other. Each player bounces on his or her toes, jockeying for position, trying to win the ball in the air with the head. This drill should be done in groups of three, with players rotating through all three positions. Service is important here—the throw must be fair to both players. Points for won headers should be counted towards a final score among the three players.

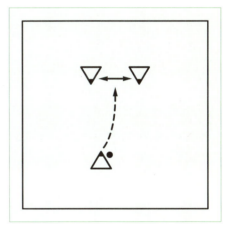

D74 **One-on-one with one goal**   Two players play against each other either with a small goal and no goalkeeper, or a large goal with a goalkeeper. Each player attempts a set number of fakes on the defender and shots on goal. Players switch roles after the set number of repetitions have been completed. The player with the most goals wins.

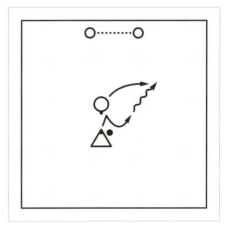

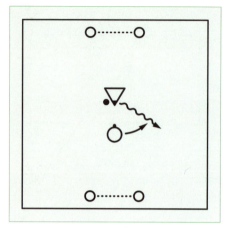

D75 One-on-one with two goals Two players play one-on-one in a confined playing area, with a small goal at each end, and given a time limit of two to four minutes to score as many goals as possible. After a short break, the game is repeated. Goals are tallied after several games. *Variation*: instead of using goals, the baselines of the playing area are used as target zones. Whenever the ball is dribbled past a line, the player gets a point.

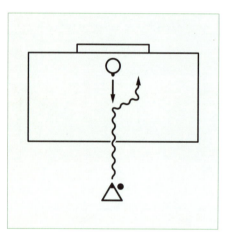

D76 Attacker vs. goalkeeper The attacker starts 25 metres from goal and tries to score by dribbling past the goalkeeper (using fakes), or by shooting.

Group offensive and defensive interactions

Teamwork

The following exercises prepare players for constantly reoccurring game situations. They serve as preparation and are performed without opponents. It is important that the players learn these skills so they are able to apply them in real games instinctively and appropriately to the situations they encounter (see **Chart 9**).

Instructional points

- Precision is more important than speed.

- The player should see the sense of the exercise, ideally, in game-related situations.

- It is not so important to do many exercises a few times, but rather a few exercises several times.

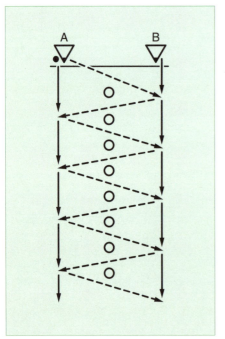

D77 **Two-player diagonal passing**   Eight to ten cones are set up in a row (one to two metres apart). One player runs along the left, the other along the right of the cones. Both pass the ball through the gaps as they run. *Variation*: the ball must be passed through each gap twice. In this situation, the gap between the cones can be increased.

Chart 9

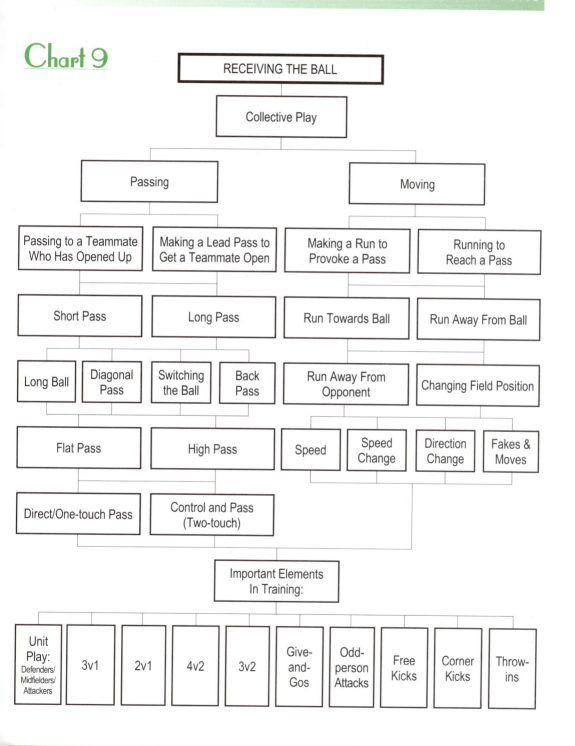

RECEIVING THE BALL

Collective Play

Passing

Moving

Passing to a Teammate Who Has Opened Up

Making a Lead Pass to Get a Teammate Open

Making a Run to Provoke a Pass

Running to Reach a Pass

Short Pass

Long Pass

Run Towards Ball

Run Away From Ball

Long Ball

Diagonal Pass

Switching the Ball

Back Pass

Run Away From Opponent

Changing Field Position

Flat Pass

High Pass

Speed

Speed Change

Direction Change

Fakes & Moves

Direct/One-touch Pass

Control and Pass (Two-touch)

Important Elements In Training:

Unit Play:
Defenders/
Midfielders/
Attackers

3v1

2v1

4v2

3v2

Give-and-Gos

Odd-person Attacks

Free Kicks

Corner Kicks

Throw-ins

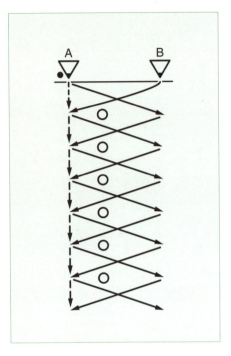

D78 Forward pass and diagonal run Six to eight cones are set up in a row eight to ten metres apart. Player A kicks the ball forward so it arrives parallel to the first of the cones, just as player B arrives, and then runs to the other side. Player B runs over to get the ball and passes it in the same direction, so it arrives parallel to the next cone, just as player A arrives, and runs to the other side, etc.

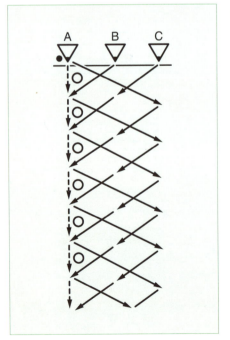

D79 Three-player passing combination Cones are set up in a row eight to ten metres apart. Three players perform the following combination: player A passes the ball forward, between the first two cones, just as player B arrives. Player B moves forward diagonally, receives the ball from player A, and passes forward so it lands between the next two cones, just as player C arrives. Player A runs to the furthest lane and player C runs into the middle lane.

D80 **Ball between the cones** As in   , the ball is again played forward, but this time through the middle, between two rows of cones, beginning with player B. After each pass, the players change positions as shown.

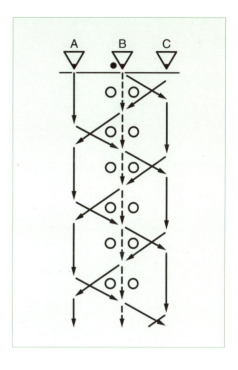

D81 **Expecting the pass** Cones are set up in a row five metres apart, over a distance of 60 metres. Two players play the ball alternately with a forward pass (parallel to the cones) and a diagonal pass (between two cones). Each player runs to the position where the next pass is expected, after passing the ball.

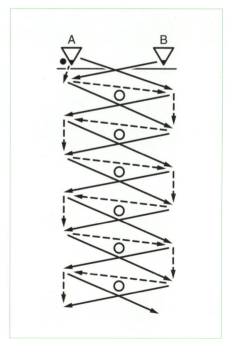

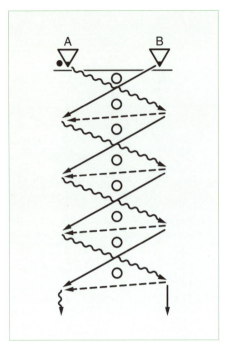

D82 Dribbling diagonally through Cones are set up in a row five metres apart, over a distance of 70 metres. Two players stand eight metres away from one another at the first cone. They begin the following combination: player A dribbles the ball diagonally through two cones to the other side, then passes the ball between cones two and three over to player B, who runs to the other side to receive the ball. Player B repeats the same pattern, and passes the ball to player A. The rule here is: when the ball starts on the right, dribble to the left, play to the right, and vice versa.

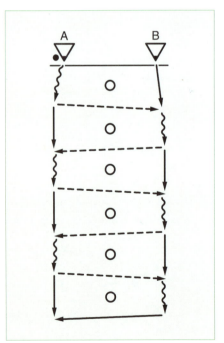

D83 Passing from between cones Cones are set up in a row five metres apart, over a distance of 60 metres. Two players stand eight metres away from one another at the first cone. They begin the following combination: player A dribbles the ball forward to the point between the first two cones and passes it over to player B. Player B then dribbles the ball forward to the point between the next two cones and passes it over to player A, and so on.

D84 Diagonal and lateral passing   In this diagonal and lateral passing drill for three players, the middle player runs behind the other two players. He passes the ball diagonally to them while in motion, and runs forward into space to receive their lateral passes.

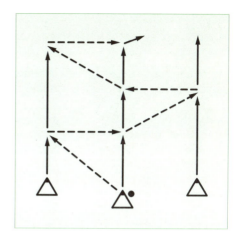

Getting open and marking

With the following exercises, teamwork and two important skills, getting open and marking, are practiced and developed.

Initially, defenders should only defend or mark passively, applying defensive strategies that allow the other team to work on their offensive skills. Only when attackers have reached a level where they attack well together, should defenders be asked to be active markers.

Instructional points for attackers

- Offensive creativity is built on the players' knowledge of basic offensive tactics.

- Attackers should take chances when moving forward, but should not take unrealistic risks.

- Players should maximize both teamwork and individual skills when moving forward.

- Players should be aware of their own abilities and those of their teammates when planning a move.

- Change of pace plays an important role in running with and without the ball.

Instructional points for defenders

- Defenders should always play "goal-side" (i.e., a defender should stand between the opponent and his or her own goal).

- Defenders should always try to keep the player with the ball to the outside, and away from the goal area.

- Defenders should always cover the most dangerous opponent when there are too many players to mark in one area.

- Defenders should always keep an eye on the ball as well as attacking players when the opposing team is moving forward.

D85a **Three-on-one possession game**   Three attackers try to keep the ball away from one defender as long as possible. The ball carrier cannot beat the defender one-on-one. The focus is to get into optimal position to receive a pass. When the defender wins the ball, his or her place is taken by the player committing the error. This drill works on getting open, staying open, and using space effectively. Since the opponent can confront only one of the three players at a time (the ball carrier), the other two must always be in position to receive a pass—ideally, "square" to (in a straight line with) the player with the ball.

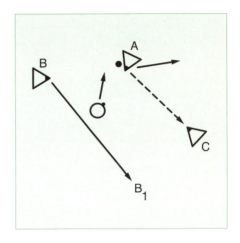

D85b **Goalkeeper attacks**   Three-on-one, with the goalkeeper as the player who defends. The 'keeper' can apply all of his goalkeeping techniques to get the ball. The field should be kept small. The ball carrier should only pass the ball when the goalkeeper confronts him. This drill will put much more pressure on the three attackers of the ball than the previous drill because the goalkeeper will have the advantage of using an extra set of limbs—his or her arms—and will have more facility with diving at the feet of the ball carriers.

D86 **Four-on-two**   This drill allows players to practice getting open. The challenge for a group of four attackers is to create three possible ball-passing opportunities, when the defenders can only cover two. Again, the best strategy for the free players is to move into position for a square ball, which makes it difficult for the two defending players to cover effectively. The defending players should be instructed to converge on the ball carrier, which forces the attacking players to find open space to receive a pass.

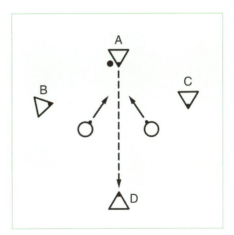

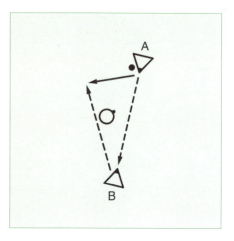

D87 **"Give-and-go" get open** The player in possession of the ball must find open space immediately after he or she has passed the ball. For the two players in possession to succeed, they must be in constant motion and communicate well. The man in possession is not allowed to beat the defending player one-on-one, as this drill emphasizes the art of getting open.

Wing play

Appropriate use of wing play is vital to any team's attacking philosophy. Not only is it often the fastest way into an opponent's defensive zone, either via a dribble or a long ball to be run onto by a winger, but it also allows a team to introduce variety into a possession game where the ball will spend a good deal of time in the central area of the field.

Instructional points

- Coaches should ensure that all players, regardless of their position, experience the wing, as it will later give the team's system some flexibility in terms of the way players move on the field and exchange positions.

- Emphasis should be placed on dribbling, fakes, and give-and-go passing, versus a long ball played down the wing.

- Players should be instructed that not every ball need be crossed from the wing, and that short passes to teammates moving into space can provide important variety to team play.

- Players should be instructed to use a variety of crosses beyond the typical cross that gets looped in towards the penalty spot. The coach could give instructions for specific crosses: near post; penalty spot; far post; driven cross; floated cross, etc.

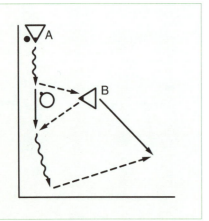

D88 **Towards the cone** Player A dribbles the ball carefully towards the cone or passive defender. Just before reaching the defender, the ball is passed to player B (who stands five metres to the side) and player A sprints past the defender. Player B passes the ball back on the first-touch. *Variation*: player A dribbles the ball to the cone. Just before reaching it, he or she fakes a pass to player B (five metres to the side), who also fakes receiving the ball, and player A darts forward down the wing with a sudden change of pace.

D89 **Towards the opponent** Player A dribbles the ball slowly towards a defender. Player B off to the side runs quickly into position behind the defender. Player A fakes a pass to the outside of the defender, and then quickly dribbles the ball to the inside and towards the goal, finishing with a shot.

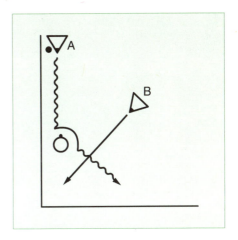

D90 **Passing behind the opponent** Player A passes the ball to player B, who runs behind the defender after faking a move to the inside, while player A runs in front of the defender after faking a move to the outside. The result is a cross-over between player A and player B. Player B runs down the wing ready to cross the ball into the box, while player A runs into the box, ready for the cross.

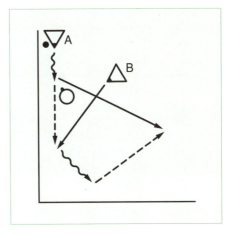

D91 **Two-on-two** Player A dribbles the ball slowly towards the defender. Player B, eight to ten metres off to the side, fakes a sprint to receive the ball, runs immediately behind his or her own marker, receives the pass from player A, and runs towards the goal for a shot.

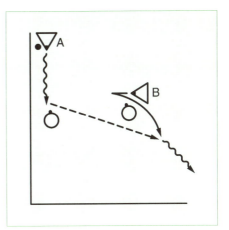

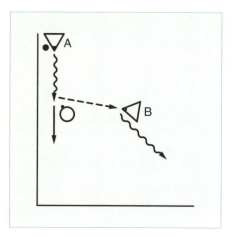

D92 **Give-and-go fake, dribble, shot** Player A dribbles the ball slowly towards the defender. Just before reaching the defender, he or she passes the ball to player B to the side (five metres away), and runs quickly behind the defender to receive a give-and-go pass. Player B fakes the give-and-go and dribbles the ball to the inside towards the goal, for a shot.

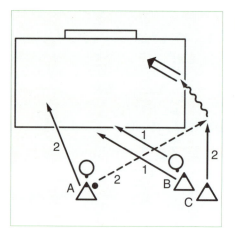

D93 **Full-flight shooter** Centre forward A dribbles the ball to the half-way line. Wing player B runs to the inside and is pursued by his or her marker. Player C quickly fills the empty space left by player B and gets the ball from player A in full flight. Player C either shoots on goal or crosses the ball into player A, who continues to advance into the 18-yard box.

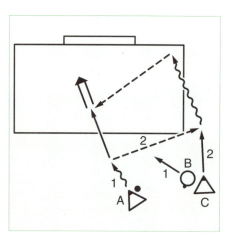

D94 **Cut back to the continuing runner** Midfielder A runs from his or her position towards the penalty spot, dribbling the ball. Defender B, who should be covering winger C, is drawn towards the middle by the player with the ball. With a diagonal pass, player A plays the ball to player C, who dribbles sharply to the goal line, and cuts the ball back to player A, who continues his or her run into the box. Player A will have an opportunity for a first-time shot on goal, such as a header.

D95 **Filling space, cutting back** Midfielder A, in a position behind the other players, dribbles the ball. Wing player B, followed by his or her marker, gets open to receive the ball. Player C quickly fills the space left by player B. Player C receives the ball from player A, runs to the goal line, and crosses the ball back into the box, targeting either player A or player B.

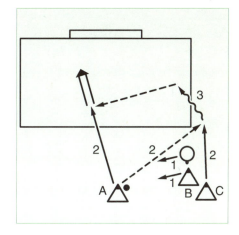

D96 **Full motion cross** Midfielder A has the ball. Winger B, covered by a defender, and in the same area as A, sprints down the wing towards the goal line to receive the ball from player A while in full motion. He or she either attempts a shot on goal, or crosses the ball into the penalty area for player A.

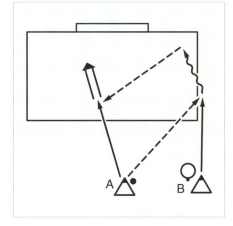

Odd-person attacks

Creating odd-person situations is an important way to create better opportunities for a successful attack.

Instructional points for attackers

• The attack must happen very quickly, so the opponents cannot change their numbers and get players back into position.

• The player who finishes the sequence of offensive maneuvers must be sufficiently open to take a shot on goal.

• Attacking players must be far away from each other so defenders can only cover one player at a time.

• The player in possession should always pass the ball when being attacked by defenders. When no defender tries to attack, he or she should attempt a shot on goal.

• During an odd-person attack, players should not try to beat a player one-on-one.

• During an odd-person attack, attackers should not perform position changes.

Instructional points for defenders

• By running back and defending the goal area, defenders should try to delay the attack (by "holding up" their marks and not diving into tackles), so more teammates can get back to help.

• In the area that is dangerous for shots on goal (approximately 20 metres away), defenders must switch to one-on-one marking. The player in possession is the most important player to mark, followed by the player holding the most dangerous position relative to the goal.

D97 Three-on-one pass-off Attacker A (middle) dribbles the ball towards the goal at a fast pace. When attacked by the defender, he or she passes the ball to the right, or to the left. If not confronted by the defender, player A will shoot on goal.

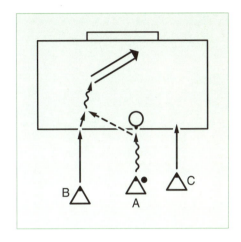

D98 Three-on-one from the outside Player A dribbles the ball from an outer position. When the defender attacks, player A passes the ball to one of the other two players, or shoots the ball on goal.

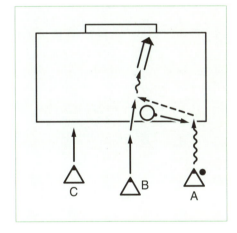

D99 Near-post—far post Attacker A dribbles the ball toward the near post with maximum pace. Attacker B runs at the same pace towards the far post. When player A is confronted by a defender, he or she passes the ball behind the defender, to player B, who shoots on goal.

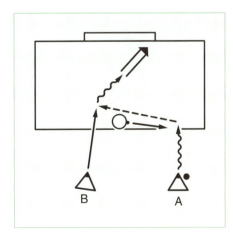

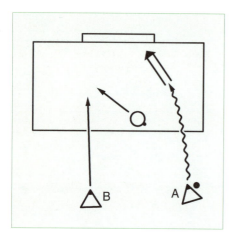

D100 <u>Shooter not attacked</u> When player A is not attacked, he or she attempts a shot on goal.

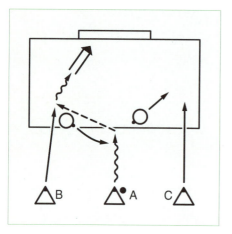

D101 <u>Three-on-two maximum pass-off</u> Attacker A dribbles the ball towards the goal with maximum pace. The ball is passed to the left or right, depending on which player remains uncovered.

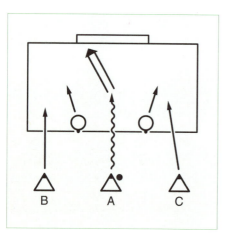

D102 <u>Two covered, one free</u> When both defenders cover the two other players, attacker A shoots on goal. The free player always takes a shot on goal.

D103 **Timed outside run**   Attacker A dribbles the ball from an outside position. When a defender is forced to make a move, player A passes the ball off to a teammate, such as player C, who times an onside run behind his or her marker. Or, if player A is not confronted by a defender, he or she shoots on goal at the best opportunity.

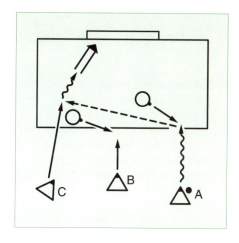

D104 **Outside and behind**   Attacker A dribbles the ball from an outside position. When a defender is forced to make a move, he or she passes the ball off to a teammate, such as player B, who may be the closer or more open man. However, if player B does not have an open shot, he or she will look for player C to make an onside run behind his or her marker for a shot on goal.

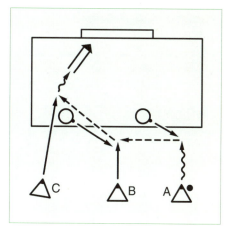

Practice games for developing team play

With the games presented in this section, most of the important principles of soccer can come into play without special instructions from the coach. However, the coach should still monitor the quality of play and ensure that players are working well together. The coach can also impose some conditions on drills and game situations, to help shape the quality of play. Such conditions include: wide-open play; two-touch soccer; height restrictions for the flight of the ball; mandatory shooting on goal after the first touch; one-on-one marking; zone defence; offside traps, etc.

Instructional points

- Ensure that players remain focused on making precise passes.

- Ensure that players adhere to ball-possession soccer.

- While these games do foster competitiveness, the coach should stop play when basic skill principles are not adhered to.

- Ensure that all balls that go out of play come back into play quickly, and that all players remain in constant motion and have constant stimulation.

D105 **Two-on-two with one goal** This is a game with one goal and a goalkeeper. This game is good for practicing odd-person attacks, and getting past an opponent. It is important that the player in possession of the ball gets challenged early and often. The attacks should begin within 30 metres of the goal.

D106 **Two-on-two or three-on-three with two small goals** The length of the field can be between 40 metres for two players, and up to 60 metres for three players per team. Players will benefit from working on passing combinations and 1v1 moves. Larger fields generate a stronger positive training effect on cardiovascular fitness.

D107 **Game with one goal** Two teams, with four to six players each, play with one goal occupied by a neutral goalkeeper. One team defends and the other one attacks and tries to score as many goals as possible through a set number of attempts. The play is dead when a goal is scored, the goalkeeper or the other team gets the ball, the ball goes out of play, or a rule is broken.

D108 **Game with one goal** Two teams, with four to six players each, play with one goal occupied by a neutral goalkeeper. Both teams attack and defend, depending on who has the ball. The game is set for five or ten minutes. The defending team is allowed to play full pressure at any point in time or position of the field.

D109 **Game with one goal** Two teams, with four to six players each, play against one goal occupied by a neutral goalkeeper. However, in order to give the attacking side an opportunity to work on attacking combinations, the defending team will always remove one player. Setting up odd-person situations is very useful for the development of team play. Odd-person situations occur often in games, but are not addressed often enough in training.

D110 **Game with two small goals and a smaller field, with fewer players**

Variations:

• Three-on-three, four-on-four, or five-on-five on a small field using handball goals. These games have the advantage that players get the ball often, and constantly have to participate in all aspects of the game. Players do not have the same opportunities for testing their ball skills in the traditional eleven-a-side game.

• Five-on-five, six-on-six, or seven-on-seven on half a soccer field. Small field handball goals can be used here again with excellent results. This game is more complicated than the previous game, and requires better endurance.

D111 **Game with four goals**   Two teams with six to eight players each play on half a field against one another. Each team has two goals standing on adjacent sides of the field and is able to attack two different goals. Both goals should never be left alone, and the task is to win the game using various attacking tactics.

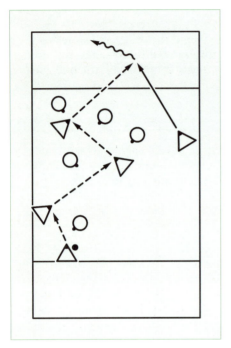

D112 **Into the end zone**   Two teams of six to eight players each play on half a field, with two end zones marked by cones. To score a point, the ball must be passed successfully to a teammate into the end zone. Before any attempted pass into the end zone, no player on either team is allowed to enter the end zone. *Variation*: the ball must be dribbled into the end zone.

PART V

SELF-DIRECTED DRILLS USING SOCCERPAL™

SoccerPal has a variety of applications, for soccer players at all levels.

For coaches who find that practice time is precious, the beauty of the SoccerPal product is that it enables players to independently work on many skills that otherwise can only be done in group sessions.

Having control over the ball using SoccerPal permits a player to target specific skill areas and to do so in a way that not only improves on individual development, but also makes it more fun. With SoccerPal on hand, the ball never leaves the player's presence; instead of the player hoping the ball will remain in his or her control after the repetition of a drill, SoccerPal assures the player that he or she will be able to do repetition after repetition. The player never has to chase a ball. As a player quickly realizes, training with SoccerPal results in many more repetitions of a skill than in any other type of drill.

For the purpose of this book, we will focus on the SoccerPal drills and principles that relate in some way to the drills that you have viewed in previous sections of this book.

Ball contact points for shooting and passing

When striking the ball it is useful to understand which parts of the ball to contact in order to make it move in a particular way. SoccerPal provides the following terminology to help players know how to execute a particular strike:

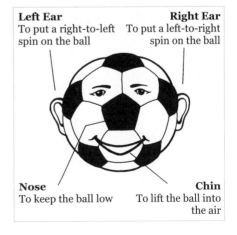

Left Ear
To put a right-to-left spin on the ball

Right Ear
To put a left-to-right spin on the ball

Nose
To keep the ball low

Chin
To lift the ball into the air

Passing the ball

D113 <u>Lace (or instep) pass</u>

- Strike the **nose** of the ball with the lower shoelaces.

- Keep the knee over the ball at impact.

- The ball should not spin.

Nose

D114 <u>Inside of the foot pass</u>

- Strike the **nose** of the ball near the arch of the foot.

- The ball should not spin.

Nose

D115 <u>Outside of the foot pass</u>

- Point the toe down and in.

- Strike the **nose** of the ball with the outer edge of the foot. Follow through.

Nose

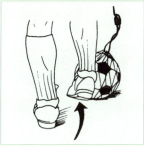

D116 <u>Chip pass</u>

Short Chip pass:

- Strike the **chin** of the ball with the lower shoelaces.

- Cut the follow-through short.

Long Chip pass:

- Strike the **chin** of ball with the lower shoelaces.

- Follow through fully.

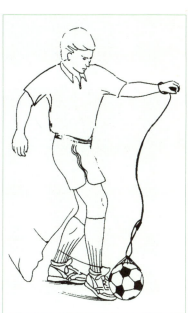

Chin

D117 <u>In-swinger pass</u>

- With the right foot: strike near the **right ear** of the ball with the lower shoelaces.

- With the left foot: strike near the **left ear** of the ball with the lower shoelaces.

- Useful for crosses from the wing.

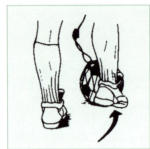

D118 <u>Out-swinger pass</u>

- With the right foot: strike near the **left ear** of the ball with the outer edge of the foot.

- With the left foot: strike near the **right ear** of the ball with the outer edge of the foot.

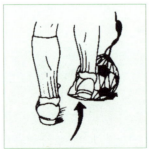

Shooting the ball

D119 <u>Laces (or instep)</u>

- Strike the ball with the lower shoelaces; keep the knee over the ball at impact.

- Depending on the desired shot, strike the **left ear**, **right ear**, **nose**, or **chin** of the ball.

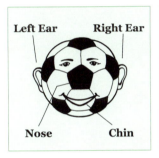

D120 <u>Inside of the foot</u>

- Strike the ball near the arch of the foot.

- Depending on the desired shot, strike the **left ear**, **right ear**, or **nose** of the ball.

D121 **Volley**

- Strike the **nose** of the ball with the lower shoelaces.
- Keep the knee over the ball at impact.

Full volley: before the ball bounces.

Half volley: after the ball bounces.

Nose

D122 **Side volley**

- Lean away from the ball at the waist. Strike the **nose** of ball with the lower shoelaces.

Nose

D123 **Bicycle kick**

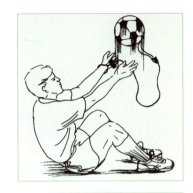

- From a seated position, throw the ball into the air directly above the feet.

- Bring the non-kicking leg up, then back down as you strike the **nose** of the ball with the lower shoelaces of the other foot.

Controlling the ball

D124 **Wedge, inside of the foot**

- Swing or pass the ball into the air.

- Track the ball to the point where it can be wedged between the ground and the inside of the foot.

D125 **Wedge, outside of the foot**

- Swing or pass the ball into the air.

- Track the ball to the point where it can be wedged between the ground and the outside of the foot.

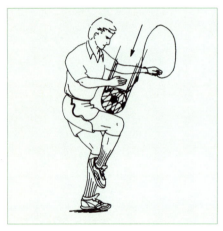

D126 **Thigh control**

- Pass the ball up above the head.

- Raise a bent leg so the thigh meets the ball at a point just above the knee.

- The ball should pop up and slightly forward.

D127 **Chest control**

- Pass the ball up above the head.

- Strike the ball with the chest angled upward and forward, leaning back from the waist.

D128 **Head control**

• Throw the ball up into the air as high as possible.

• Just before contact with the head, bend the knees and sink the hips.

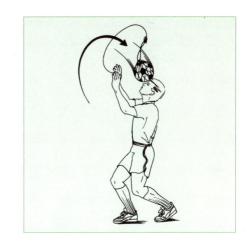

Heading the ball

D129 **Self-pendulum header**

• Keep the eyes open. Strike the **nose** of the ball with the forehead (just below the hairline).

Nose

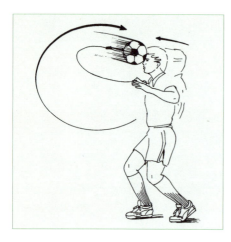

D130 **Self-toss header**

- Attack the ball by bringing the arms back and the head forward. Strike the **nose** of the ball with the forehead.

Nose

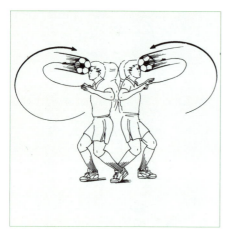

D131 **Side-to-side headers**

- Swing the ball across the body to one side.

- Turn the whole body (including the feet) towards the ball.

Nose

- Strike the **nose** of the ball with the forehead.

- Repeat.

Coaching notes

- SoccerPal is also very useful for heading drills when suspended from a soccer net crossbar or a tree.

- Simply suspend SoccerPal from a height that will require you to jump to your maximum.

- Then begin your session of endless jumping headers. The beauty of this drill, like all of the others mentioned, is that you can then practice headers on your own and not worry about chasing stray balls.

Advanced drills

D132 **Foot to heel**

- Kick the ball forward with one foot so it makes a full circle up, over, and behind the body.

- When the ball has made a full circle, kick it back with the heel of the same foot.

D133 **Left foot to right foot**

- Kick the ball with the inside of the left foot across the body so it makes a full circle and arrives on the inside of the right foot.

- After the ball has made a full circle, use the right foot to send it back to the left.

D134 **Foot to head**

- Chip the ball up to the head.

- Head the ball back down towards the feet.

- Kick the ball back up before it touches the ground.

- Keep the ball moving continuously.

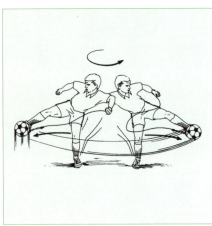

D135 **Volley side-to-side**

- Using the laces of the shoes, volley the ball across the body, side to side.

- Keep the ball moving continuously across the body as long as possible without stopping.

D136 **Shoelaces tap on one foot**

- Maintaining your balance on the planted foot, use only the laces of the other foot to gently tap the ball forward.

- These should be short, soft, controlled, continuous kicks.

- After a set number of repetitions, change feet.

D137 **Inside of the foot tap on one foot**

• Use only the inside of the foot to gently tap the ball so it moves in a circle around the stationary leg.

• These should be short, soft, controlled, continuous taps of the ball.

• The movement of the foot and ball should become rhythmical.

• After a set number of repetitions, change feet.

SoccerPal ties in nicely with the lead-up games, drills, and exercises presented in this book. It is a simple, inexpensive product that more than pays for itself in terms of the improved ball skills that result from an enormous increase in repetitions.

To get a more detailed look at the various independent drills, and to observe how SoccerPal can be used in partner or group situations, order the SoccerPal video and Player's Guide.

For more information on the SoccerPal products, visit **www.soccerpal.com**.

PART VI

CIRCUIT TRAINING

Circuit training is designed to develop soccer-specific skills and fitness. It is a training program that incorporates a number of carefully selected exercises to practice several key basketball skills in one session.

Each exercise within the circuit is numbered and referred to as a station. The player progresses from one exercise station to another in sequence, completing a prescribed amount of work (repetitions) at each station.

The selection of exercises, number of repetitions, number of stations per circuit, etc. must be suited to the participants' age, training experience, and performance ability. Furthermore, depending upon the athletes' performance levels, training phase, and training objectives, each circuit can be repeated three to six times, with rest intervals between individual circuits ranging between zero and 240 seconds.

In circuit training, the loading of the main muscle groups (prime movers) changes as the player moves from one exercise to another. The loading at each station is normally below the player's maximum, which allows the athlete to move quickly from one station to another, requiring relatively little rest between exercises. The intensity of training remains relatively high throughout the circuit, which also generates a strong positive training effect on cardiovascular fitness.

Circuit training has many valuable organizational aspects. It can accommodate a relatively large number of participants at one time, requires relatively inexpensive equipment, and can be easily adapted to the individual needs and abilities of players. Coaches have found circuit training to be an excellent form of preparation during the preparatory phase of training; but due to its time efficiency, it can also be very effective for maintaining fitness during the pre-competitive and competitive phases of training.

Athletes should be introduced to a circuit training program in a highly organized manner. The coach must explain the objectives and the potential benefits of the program, as well as outline the structure and procedures. Individual performance cards must be prepared for each participant. They are used to record the achieved results, such as times per circuit and achieved number of repetitions/points per station, etc. Proper execution of each exercise, including the proper sequence of exercising and correct method of recording the results on the individual performance cards, must be emphasized.

Several forms of circuit training exist, depending on the goals to be achieved in training. Eight different forms of circuit training are presented in this section. For more information on circuit training, refer to **Circuit Training for All Sports**, a Sport Books Publisher publication.

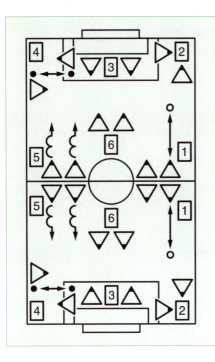

Circuit 1

Goals: To train speed, jumping endurance, upper body strength endurance, core abdominal strength, agility, as well as soccer-specific movement.

Participants: Maximum of 4 per station. This circuit can accommodate a squad of 24 players.

Expectations: The circuit is completed two to three times. The exercises are performed as quickly as possible. Players should switch stations every 40 seconds, and in more advanced training environments, every 25 to 30 seconds.

Materials: Cones, medicine balls, stopwatch.

Circuit stations:

Station 1:
   A 30-metre sprint to a cone 30 metres away at maximum speed. Return with a light jog and repeat. *Task*: 3 reps.

Station 2:
   Stomach crunches. Lying on the back, feet flat on the ground, knees bent, hands across the chest, players raise their upper body eight to ten inches off the ground, then lower it back to the ground. *Task*: 30 reps.

Station 3:
   Vertical jumps. These are simulations of headers without the ball. Emphasis is on getting maximum vertical height with jumps straight up into the air. *Task*: 10 reps.

Station 4:
   Slide tackles performed between two medicine balls ten metres apart. The medicine balls provide players with a target towards which to slide. Players should focus on slide and foot contact, as well as speed. *Variation*: the power of the slide tackle can be trained by having a partner provide resistance behind the ball. *Task*: 10 reps.

Station 5:
   Forward-thrusting head ball jumping movements, ending in a squat position. The emphasis for this station should be on the heading motion. *Task*: 10 reps.

Station 6:
   Push-ups, with an emphasis on working the chest and triceps. *Task*: 15 reps.

Circuit 2

Goals: To train starting speed, agility, jumping endurance, and soccer-specific movement.

Participants: Maximum of 4 per station. This circuit can accommodate a squad of 24 players.

Expectations: The circuit is completed two to three times. The exercises are performed as quickly as possible. Players should switch stations every 40 seconds, and in more advanced training environments, every 25 to 30 seconds.

Materials: Cones, stopwatch.

Circuit stations:

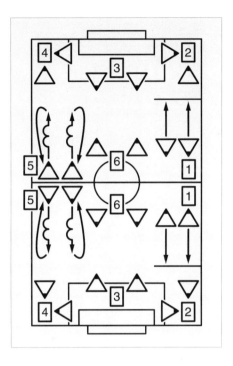

Station 1:
    Backwards sprint of ten steps. Return to starting position with light jog and repeat. *Task*: 6 reps.

Station 2:
    Push-ups with legs crossed to the left or right. *Task*: 10 reps.

Station 3:
    Stomach crunches. Lying on the back, feet flat on the ground, knees bent, hands across the chest, players raise their upper body eight to ten inches off the ground, then lower it back to the ground. *Task*: 30 reps.

Station 4:
    Reverse push-ups (for the triceps). With the body facing up (opposite of the push-up position) and legs straight out, the body is balanced on the heels and hands. When the elbows are bent and the body dips, the triceps muscles of the arms are engaged. *Task*: 10 reps.

Station 5:
    Ten forward frog jumps. Return with a light jog and repeat. *Task*: 20 reps.

Station 6:
    Alternating chest and triceps push-ups. The legs are moved between the arms in order to switch positions after every repetition. *Task*: 10 reps each.

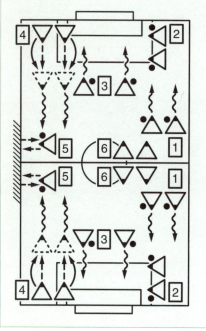

Circuit 3

Goals: To improve ball technique through high intensity repetitions and increase upper body strength.

Participants: Maximum of 4 per station. This circuit can accommodate a squad of 24 players.

Expectations: The circuit is completed two to three times. The exercises are performed as quickly as possible and as technically correct as possible. Players are should switch stations every 40 seconds, and in more advanced training environments, every 25 to 30 seconds.

Materials: Target wall, 3 to 4 pairs of dumbbells, 20 balls (four balls per station), stopwatch.

Circuit stations:

Station 1:
Participants dribble in a straight line as fast as possible for 30 metres. Return with a light jog and repeat. *Task*: 3 reps.

Station 2:
From a seated position, participants throw a ball up into the air, jump to their feet, and control the ball with the head, then the foot. *Task*: 10 reps.

Station 3:
Participants dribble five metres, fake a shot, step on the ball, and turn; repeat back to the starting position. *Task*: 10 reps.

Station 4:
The ball is thrown into the air and run on to and controlled with the instep for a short, five-metre dribble. *Task*: 10 reps.

Station 5:
Participants practice throw-ins against a target wall (five metres away) and control the ball with any body part off the rebound. *Task*: 10 reps.

Station 6:
Lying on the back, participants perform dumbbell curls (10 to 15 kg weight) in both hands. *Task*: 10 reps.

Circuit 4

Goals: To improve ball technique through high intensity repetitions.

Participants: Unlimited number of participants, although drills must be performed with a partner.

Expectations: The circuit is completed two to three times. Each participant has a partner who accompanies him or her from station to station. Partners must complete as many repetitions as possible in 30 seconds at each station. Between each station there is a 30-second break.

Materials: 1 soccer ball per pair, 2 medicine balls (1 to 3 kg), stopwatch.

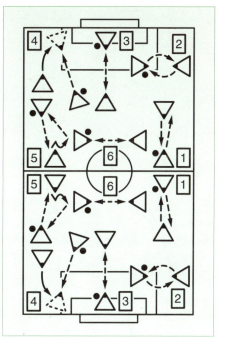

Circuit stations:

Station 1:
> One partner five metres away passes the ball on the ground to the other player, alternately to the right and left. The ball is passed back on the first touch.

Station 2:
> One partner three metres away throws a medicine ball to a seated player. The ball is thrown back to the partner with a throw-in style.

Station 3:
> One partner three metres away throws a ball to a seated player. The ball is headed back to the partner.

Station 4:
> One partner five meters away passes the ball to a player running into space. The player receives the ball, passes it back to the partner, then runs into a new space.

Station 5:
> One partner five metres away plays the ball (low) to the other player. The player performs a fake as he or she controls the ball, then passes it back to the partner.

Station 6:
> One partner five metres away throws the ball to a seated player, who must get up and play a one-touch ball back to the partner.

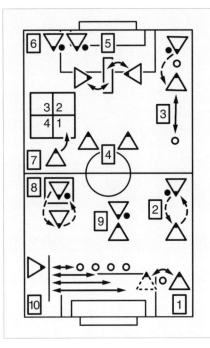

Circuit 5

Goals: To improve soccer-specific fitness.

Participants: 2 per station.

Expectations: The circuit is completed two times. Partners move together from station to station, completing as many repetitions as possible (explosively) in 30 seconds. Between each station there is a 30-second break. At the end of each circuit, participants complete a 400-metre run.

Materials: 5 medicine balls (1 to 3 kg), cones, soccer ball, tape, 2 platform boxes, whistle, stopwatch.

Circuit stations:

Station 1 (Lateral barrier jump):
  Standing beside a cone, players jump vertically and laterally over the cone, back and forth, as many times as possible.

Station 2 (Medicine ball sit-ups):
  One partner throws a medicine ball to a partner lying on the ground, who reclines back, and passes the ball back on the way up.

Station 3 (Jumping headers/Agility run):
  One partner backpedals ten metres to a cone, then runs ten metres forward and jumps up to maximal height to head a ball back to his or her partner.

Station 4 (Push-ups):
  Participants perform as many push-ups as possible until the end of the interval.

Station 5 (Jump to a box):
  Partners take a two-step approach to jump up to a box 6- to 12-inches high with two feet.

Station 6 (Trunk rotator):
  Sitting on the ground holding a medicine ball with the legs spread, participants turn to the left and place the ball behind the back. Participants then turn to the right, pick up the ball, bring it around to the left side, place the ball behind the back, and so on.

Station 7 (Single-leg pattern jumps):
  A square with four sections is marked. Participants jump with the right leg diagonally from section 1 to 3, then switch to the left leg and jump from section 2 to 4.

Station 8 (Vertical toss):
  One partner stands on a box and drops a medicine ball to a partner sitting with his or her back to the box. The ball is caught and passed back over the head to the partner.

Station 9 (Superman toss):
  One partner drops a medicine ball to a partner lying the stomach. The ball is caught with the outstretched hands and returned to the standing partner.

Station 10 (Shuttle run):
  Participants run back and forth between four pylons laid out ten yards apart.

Circuit 6

Goals: To improve abdominal and leg strength using medicine balls.

Participants: Maximum of 2 players per station. This circuit can accommodate a squad of 20 players.

Expectations: The circuit is completed twice. Partners move from station to station, completing as many repetitions as possible in 30 seconds. Between each station there is a 30-second break.

Materials: 20 medicine balls suitable to the age and level of participants (1 to 3 kg), stopwatch.

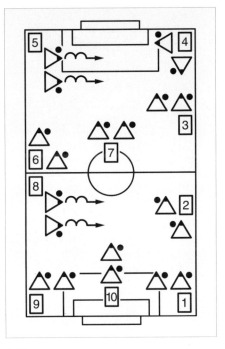

Circuit stations:

Station 1 (Ball lunges):
> From a throw-in stance with a medicine ball behind the head, players alternate lunging forward with either leg (bending no more than 90°).

Station 2 (Squat bounces):
> Holding a medicine ball above the head, players squat and lower the ball out in front with straight arms.

Station 3 (Leg to ball):
> Lying flat on the back with a medicine ball held out above the chest, players raise the legs to touch the ball with the feet and return to the starting position.

Station 4 (Ball extensions):
> Seated with knees bent and arms stretched behind for support, players hold a medicine ball between the ankles. The knees are extended to a high diagonal position and lowered.

Station 5 (Squat hops):
> Holding a medicine ball with both hands, players perform short forward hops in a squat position (knees bent less than 90°).

Station 6 (Leg raises):
> Lying flat on the back, players perform leg raises with a medicine ball held between the ankles. The ball is lifted straight up above the head and lowered.

Station 7 (Ball lifts):
> Seated with legs straight holding a medicine ball with the ankles and arms stretched behind for support, players lift the ball and twist the trunk alternately to the left and right.

Station 8 (Ankle squat hops):
> Same as Station 5, except the ball is held between the ankles.

Station 9 (Ball lunges):
> Repeat Station 1 (ball lunges).

Station 10 (Partner ball sit-ups):
> From a straddle stance with a medicine ball held behind the neck, participants bend forward with a flat back and return to the starting position.

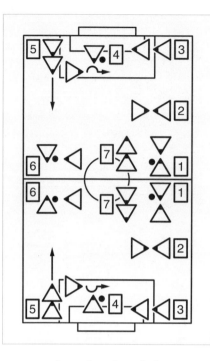

Circuit 7

Goals: To improve leg strength and ball technique through partner exercises.

Participants: Maximum of 2 players per station. This circuit can accommodate a squad of 20 players.

Expectations: The circuit is completed twice. Partners move from station to station, completing as many repetitions as possible in 30 seconds. Between each station there is a 30-second break.

Materials: 3 SoccerPals, stopwatch.

Circuit stations:

Station 1 (Bicycle kicks):
>   One partner suspends a SoccerPal above the other partner, who performs bicycle kicks lying on his or her back.

Station 2 (Straddle resistance):
>   One player lies on his or her back and raises straight legs to an angled position. A partner stands at the player's feet, grasps them from the inside, and forces the stretched legs to a wide straddle position, applying continual pressure. Keeping the trunk and pelvis on the ground, the bottom player resists the pressure as he or she attempts to close the legs.

Station 3 (Jumping against partner resistance):
>   Partners stand behind one another. The front player bends one leg at the knee. The back player holds the raised foot or ankle with both hands. The front player then tries to jump a specific distance against even resistance by his or her partner.

Station 4 (Diving headers):
>   A partner holds a SoccerPal (adjusted to the shortest length) 30 to 90 centimetres off the ground. The other partner dives to head the ball from a kneeling position with the arms reaching forward for a controlled landing.

Station 5 (Running against partner resistance):
>   One partner stands behind the other and pushes him or her with both hands against even resistance.

Station 6 (Volley with a partner):
>   A partner holds a SoccerPal (waist height), while the other partner performs repeated side volleys using the instep.

Station 7 (Leg extensions with a partner):
>   One player lies on his or her back with legs pulled in to the chest. A partner places the chest or back on the soles of the feet, keeping the body completely straight. The tips of the toes or knees should be touching the ground. The lead partner then straightens both legs simultaneously and brings them back to the initial position.

Circuit 8

Goals: To improve ball skills.

Participants: 2 to 4 per station.

Expectations: At each station, players must perform a certain number of repetitions. Players change constantly from station to station, until each station has been done twice.

Materials: 1 ball per player, 5 cones for a dribbling segment, a target wall.

Circuit stations:

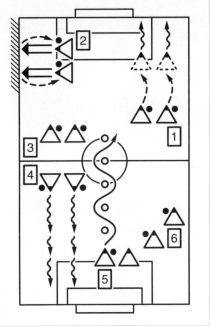

Station 1:
    Players throw the ball into the air and run on to it for a controlled, five-metre dribble. *Task*: 15 reps.

Station 2:
    Players shoot against a target wall five metres away, followed by ball reception. Start with the non-dominant leg, then repeat with the dominant leg. *Task*: 15 reps.

Station 3:
    Players juggle a ball with the head. *Task*: 50 reps without interruption.

Station 4:
    Players dribble the ball, fake a shot, then pull back with the sole and turn. The action is repeated back towards the starting position. *Task*: 15 reps.

Station 5:
    Players continuously dribble a ball around five cones, three metres apart. *Task*: 3 reps.

Station 6:
    Players juggle a ball with the feet. *Task*: 50 reps without interruption.

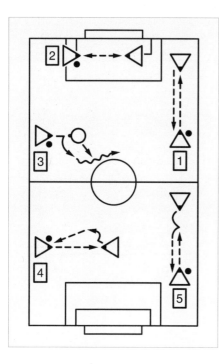

Circuit 9

Goals: To improve ball skills.

Participants: 2 to 4 per station.

Expectations: Each pair practices at each station for one minute per partner, then everyone switches to the next station without a break. The exercises should be performed swiftly, but technically correct. Participants perform 2 to 4 circuits.

Materials: 1 ball per pair, stopwatch.

Circuit stations:

Station 1:
>   Partner 1 five metres away throws the ball in, partner 2 plays it back with one touch.

Station 2:
>   Both partners three metres apart pass the ball with their heads, keeping the ball up without interruption.

Station 3:
>   Partner 1 five metres away dribbles and uses a double fake to get past partner 2, who provides only passive resistance; the dribble is continued for five metres.

Station 4:
>   Partner 1 five metres away passes a low ball to partner 2. Partner 2 controls the ball, adds a fake, and passes the ball back.

Station 5:
>   Partner 1 five metres away throws the ball to partner 2. Partner 2 jumps and heads the ball back.

Notes